BOWLING

Introduction

ONE OF the things about athletes that fascinates people the most is the part about "When did you decide to become this or that," or, "When did you first begin to notice that you had a special talent . . . and what did you do about it . . . and who encouraged you?"

I really don't believe there is any such thing as an ideal time to get started in anything, and by that I mean baseball or football or electronics or bowling. Some people don't express an interest in any sport or other endeavor until they mature somewhat, while with other people circumstances dictate what they'll be and how good they'll be at it. In my case I can illustrate very easily how it all began, because it started long before I was ever really aware of it.

My dad owned a bowling center in Saint Louis, and ever since I could understand the words that older folks spoke I knew that my father was a great one. Anyhow, because the family was in the business, naturally my dad pushed me toward the game, just the same way, I guess, that Mickey Mantle's dad envisioned the day that his kid would become a major-league star.

I've been told that I was only three years old when I went bowling for the first time. Since the ball was much too big for me to lift and the pins much too difficult for me to hit, the pinboys—yes, there were pinboys then—in what seemed to me for a long time to be an effort to build up my confidence but that I realize now was actually a way for them to curry favor with the boss, my dad— gave me a ball ordinarily used for duckpins and lined up pins in each of the gutters. This meant that the ball I threw, which always wound up in one of the two gutters, was sure to knock down something every time.

Though I spent many an hour at the lanes and tossed the equivalent of thousands of games, I really didn't get around to serious bowling until I was a teenager—albeit a young one. I was thirteen when I joined a league and became part of the

4

American Junior Bowling Congress. I loved the thrill of competition, and I had an advantage over my fellow bowlers. In the back of my mind, there was always that comforting feeling that any time something developed in my game that wasn't to my liking, or if I felt that something in my game needed steady work, I could always go back to my dad's place and practice—free of charge and with the most expert instruction anyone could ever want. Don't forget—my dad was a star in the thirties and forties and was particularly good in match play. He's a Hall of Famer now, but I really think he eased his way into retirement much too soon because of the lack of competition in Saint Louis in those days.

When I was born, in 1942, it's almost as if my father decided right then and there that someone else had come along to carry on the name of Burton in the game we both love so much. He was too smart to let me in on his plans—plans, that is, for my becoming a great bowler. He waited for me to come to him, and when I did I had already developed a style, some elements of which didn't sit too well with him. At the outset he pointed out two basic errors I was making, mistakes he considered ruinous to a good game. First of all, I used to turn sideways at the line on the release, and second, I was like most other new bowlers in believing that in order to be a good bowler I had to toss a great big hook.

If any of you out there need some starting point from which to get your game in hand and be on your way toward big scores, maybe you ought to burn those two items into your mind. Face the pins on delivery and forget about that roundhouse curve.

My father stressed these points at the outset and he continued to harp on them. He told me to concentrate all my efforts on accuracy and footwork. There was no compromise for each, he said, and each played equal roles in the improvement of a bowler's game. I've been bowling in pretty good company for many years now, and I've never had any trouble either with getting the ball into the strike area or with my footwork. Of course, when I mention the word "footwork" it almost goes without saying that I mean timing.

I've been asked by reporters and other bowlers to reveal just what there is about my game that sets me apart from others. When I say what I'm about to say it's not that I'm immodest—it's just that when I believe something I cannot mince words. I think the strongest part of my game is my footwork, and I also think my footwork is as good as anybody's. My armswing? That's something else. It could stand improvement, and I will spend much time working on that part of my game. Putting it another way, it isn't so vital for you to be great in many areas—the thing to avoid is a major fault, or faults, in your game. I don't have any in my game and that's why I've had so much success.

I have tried to get all facets of my game into such good working order that no condition or circumstance I run into on the tour will stop me. I don't care if the condition is fast or slow or up or down or in and out—they can't come up with an angle I can't play and can't play well. If you look at the averages you'll see that I've been either the leader or right near the lead the past few years. I even had one streak of a few years' standing during which I never shot for under a 200 average at a tournament. But as I said, I state these items only because they help prove a point and because they make me feel more than qualified to tell the millions of bowlers who can't get going with their bowling scores just what to do.

Before we get going—before we start working on your game—I want to mention once again what I know to be the two most important aspects of the game, accuracy and timing (footwork).

Once you've got your footwork down pat you graduate to the next plateau, which is putting the ball where you want it. I compare it somewhat to baseball, where you have a million guys who can toss the ball hard but only a handful who can get it over the plate. By the time you get through this book you should know where the ball is going all the time, and at the same time you'll know where you are going in the game.

When everything else falls into place, it's only natural that the finishing touch will be there. We'll cover all phases of bowling, with an eye toward the big payoff—the strike—on each and every shot. And when that fails, we'll teach you how to do the next best thing, which is to make those spares.

Fundamentals

THE SUPREME ACHIEVEMENT in bowling is a 300 game—twelve strikes in a row and immortality. But to resurrect a very old line, you can't get them all unless you get the first. So, let's state here and now that the ultimate in bowling is the strike—that delicious feeling that comes only when you see all ten pins fall on your first try each frame. Before and after the strike, however, there will be countless hours of fun and excitement and the thrill of competing with and against those who bowl better than you whom you beat, and those who have less ability than you but still manage to whip you once in a while.

The objects of the game are as simple or as complicated as you care to make them. If you're a physical fitness cultist you can get more than a fair share of exercise just by bowling many games. If you're introverted bowling could be the way out. If you're extroverted there's no need describing the many ego trips you can take. The very foundation of the game is built on teamwork and accomplishment, the dividends being the fun and excitement I spoke about and will probably touch upon again as we go on.

I've never bought the line, "you don't have to be good at a game to get full enjoyment out of it." The key word there is "full." You can have a good enough time at bowling by doing reasonably well on occasion, but no one has ever lived who was content with mediocrity, who didn't grit his teeth in anguish when he wanted to do better and didn't have the equipment. I don't know of anyone who ever took a job and from that moment was happy to make the same amount of money year after year while never altering his function. People just aren't built that way, a concept you can easily transfer to sports. If you've gotten four strikes in a row, you desperately want a fifth. And if you've gone four frames without getting a strike, you're even more desperate to make your first.

Have fun while you bowl, but never, ever lose sight of the goal—a strike on every shot, a perfect game every time you complete ten frames. If you adopt that philosophy you'll wind up winning more games than the fellow next to you and you'll have a lifetime of gratification, for there is no game that offers as much self-satisfaction as bowling.

Unlike a hole-in-one in golf, where you never know the ball has fallen into the cup until you get to the green, the perfect game in bowling is the end result of twelve straight heart-pounding, palms-perspiring, spine-tingling strikes, each of which is immediately there for you and your teammates and the world to see.

Unlike so many other games, you don't need a cart or a porter or a device of any kind to help you carry the tools of the trade. Of course, later on in your game, as your scores and sophistication begin to climb, you may avail yourself of some rather interesting equipment. But you can start out simply and you can stay that way forever and ever. As a matter of fact, you really don't need anything. You can put this book down right now, walk into the neighborhood bowling center, and start bowling with the ball the man will lend you. The only expenditure you will have is the cost of a game of bowling and the small fee for rental of bowling shoes, which you must wear. Other than that . . . nothing.

You should, however, as soon as you have the time and the money and the basics of the game down pat, get your own bowling ball and shoes (the latter because in the long run it will be less expensive). Your own ball serves a dual purpose, giving you a precision instrument with which to do the job in the proper manner as well as building your ego. Yes, it's true—nothing makes the bowler feel more like a bowler than trotting out his very own bowling ball when the league starts up.

After you have these two items—ball and shoes—you can start adding to your list, but you'll need only simple little things then. A towel will come in handy if your hands perspire excessively, and you may want a little wire brush to make sure your bowling shoes pick up no foreign matter. Again, I hasten to point out that none of those items are really necessary to your game.

No doubt you've been advised by others as to what you should or should not wear. Along these lines I can only say that you should never wear any kind of restrictive apparel while bowling. By that I mean don't try to bowl while wearing tight pants or a tight shirt. Except for a few bowlers who are very style conscious, just about all of the pros compete in short-sleeved shirts to give them maximum freedom of armswing. The only fellow I know of who has ever departed from that rule is a well-dressed star who made the televised finals of Pro Bowlers Tour a few years back and wore a shirt with those big, wide bell sleeves. He looked great, and I'm not implying that the sleeves inhibited his smooth swing in any way, but he lost the title when he missed a crucial spare late in the game. So, with clothing, let common sense be your guide. You'd have to be pretty vain about your dressing habits to want to wear anything that might possibly keep you from doing your very best. There are enough things to worry about in improving your game without adding unnecessary woes.

The last time I took count, there were about ten thousand bowling establishments throughout the United States. If you have the time and the desire, you may bowl at any or all of them. Bowling centers are open to everyone; the only problem may be in getting to bowl when you want to bowl. The lifeblood of just about every operation is league bowling, and bowling proprietors give their all in organizing and then keeping leagues. League revenue is guaranteed income for the proprietor, and it's only right that he funnel most of his energy toward making available to his customers a varied and interesting slate of leagues. These may be two-, three-, four-, or even five-man leagues, or they may even be singles competitions. There should be leagues for low-average bowlers, as well as for those with middle and high averages. If you want to make a go of being a bowling proprietor—take my word for it, it's really big business—you have to offer something for everyone. That means men and women, boys and girls, young and old. And you've got to keep your place humming for as many hours as is possible for as many days of the week as you can.

What this all adds up to is a maximum amount of places and opportunities for you and yours to go bowling. You should attempt to join a league as soon as you can, and don't buy any suggestion from anyone that you should wait until you get really good before joining one. You'll start bowling better almost immediately once you're part of a formal league, for the simple reason that there'll be more incentive for you to do better when others are depending on your performance. So by all means sign up today—if today's the day they're signing up league bowlers. Remember, though—league bowling is infectious. Odds are that once you climb aboard you're there to stay for the rest of your life. And that's the way it's supposed to be, because bowling's a lifetime game.

Of course, once you've become a league bowler you don't have to stop there. Usually in the early evening hours, or late at night, or on weekends, there are lanes set aside for "open" play. That means, simply, that there's no league activity going on. This is the time for you to try that new delivery or that new ball or to experiment with a different release. This is the right time to make adjustments, or determine that none is needed. It's still fun time for you, without the consequences of missing a critical spare or failing to come up with a key "double" when your teammates are depending on you.

You'll find that, once you've gotten your feet wet and are starting to bowl on a somewhat regular basis, many other avenues will be open to you. You may enter tournaments on your own or you and your buddies can enter one as a unit. Bowling proprietors are usually clannish, and they'll help spread the word on a nearby tournament to keep your interest in the game at a high pitch. In several cities newspapers sponsor tournaments, and quite often you and your teammates will find yourselves traveling to a far-off place to compete. And you'll soon discover that even though you eat, breathe, and sleep bowling you'll not be able to partake of all the events and tournaments and "specials" you'll read about or hear about at your local bowling center.

Starting Out

ASSUMING THAT MOST bowlers will really get into the game once they've reached their teens —I mean about thirteen or fourteen—although it is probable that they have hardly ever gone bowling before that, there are some basic bits of information I'd like to pass along. If you're thirteen or so you're probably not the size of a full-grown man, which means you haven't reached maximum strength. If that's the case, do as I did —try and find a ball that weighs no more than thirteen or fourteen pounds, or even lighter than that if you're slightly built, as I was. I didn't grow to full adult size until I got out of the service. I think I was about five-five or five-six and really skinny when I decided to get serious about the game, and I always tried to find the lightest ball on the rack when I didn't have my own handy.

From that point, the next logical thing is to learn how to move your feet so you get into a smooth delivery and are able to deliver the ball without falling all over yourself—maybe even hurting yourself. Though there are variations, you should start out by learning the four-step approach. And if you find that it gets results and that you are showing a steady and impressive improvement in your game, there really is no reason in the world why you should ever try any other method of delivery. Learn the four-step and be able to lift and swing the ball in a safe and comfortable fashion. These are the first two points I'd like to make and like you to retain.

The first objective is to get your timing and footwork down to a science, and you just can't do it with a ball that's too heavy. (Incidentally, I'd better mention something right here before I get taken to task for telling you to find the lightest ball you can. At our bowling center in Saint Louis we have balls that are as light as six pounds —we call them "six-shooters," but they're only for tiny kids who can push, not lift, a ball. When I say light, I mean in the range of twelve to fourteen pounds.) If you're on the small side and try to roll a sixteen-pound ball you'll run into instant trouble, because the weight of the ball will undoubtedly make you turn sideways at the line, and if you remember what I told you at the start, you've got to face the pins squarely at the point of release. And don't be fearful about getting too used to a light ball; if you're of reasonable size you'll graduate to a heavier ball after a hundred games or so, because by then you'll have the basics down pat and you'll find the rhythm that is so necessary.

If I have a pupil who is starting out cold I watch him toss a few shots before making any determinations or giving any advice. Oh, I'll put him in the right direction by telling him to stand somewhat to the right on the approach while looking at the pins. Even if the student tells me someone else has advised him to stand in the center of the approach and to pick out a spot on the lane, I steer him from this tack. You don't learn to run without learning to walk first, and neophyte bowlers don't spot-bowl or stand smack in the middle on the approach.

I've seen so many bowlers, even some who have gotten up to a fair average, who do everything terribly wrong. They flail their arms and rush up to the line, instead of walking, and they just heave the ball. It's evident to me that they never learned how at the beginning, and because they didn't they kept bad habits. Sure, you can get your average up to some respectable plateau by doing the wrong things, but just think of how far you can go when you try doing things the right way. I'd rather teach a first-timer the essential points than work with someone who has spent years and years doing everything improperly.

This is why, when I'm working with a raw pupil, I'll show him what to do. I'll exaggerate the four steps by walking quite slowly to the foul line, and I'll stop at each of the steps to indicate where the ball should be positioned at each step. I stress that the first step and the pushaway are most important, because everything that follows flows from that initial movement. I'll walk with a pupil to the line and guide his feet and his arm. You'd be surprised at how soon, by repetition, the movements start becoming second nature.

I'll go on record with this statement: Show me a youngster who is reasonably coordinated and who has learned the importance of that first step— either by having had it drummed into him or by reading a book such as this—and I'll show you a bowler who after as little as forty games will be shooting for a 120 average. Maybe that doesn't sound too high to you, but take my word for it—if you don't learn at all, or if you learn wrong, it can be a pretty tough mark to hit.

Once a bowler, and I don't mean to imply that all new bowlers have to be young bowlers, has reached an average of somewhere around 120 and has a fair number of games under his belt, that's the time for him to seek out a competent instructor and attempt to move his game to another level.

I'll tell you a story that will indicate quite well the way a person can become anything he wants to be, providing he's diligent enough and cares enough and is honest with himself.

I remember a fellow back in Saint Louis—I guess he was in his mid-twenties—who wanted desperately to become a good bowler. Oh, he was pretty good, shooting in the 190s, but that wasn't enough. Well, while he didn't have enough money to go bowling whenever he wanted to, he also knew that in bowling—just as in business—if you want to succeed you have to work at it. And since he was a carpenter, he got himself a pile of wood and in one corner of his bedroom he set up his own approach. That's right—he built an approach, regulation length, made a backstop, and then put a floor-length mirror at the end.

He'd get out his bowling ball, put on his shoes,

and hour after hour after hour, go through all the motions required. He'd toss the ball against the backstop, observe how he looked in the mirror, then go out to the padding and retrieve the ball to get ready for another shot.

I'm not saying this for effect, only because it's the truth. The last time I saw this fellow bowling league he was averaging around 210, and I'll go on record as saying that he had the smoothest footwork and timing I've ever seen. He proved to himself and everyone else that there's more than one way to skin a cat. He just couldn't afford to pay money to practice at a bowling center, but he found another way and it paid off for him. Of course, what he did was a bit way out—building a miniature lane, so to speak—but what he did serves as an object lesson for all of us, especially in bowling. Practice may not make perfect, but it makes all of us better bowlers.

Once the bowler has learned the necessary functions of footwork and timing—and he should have those two things pretty much down pat once he's hit the 140 mark—the natural impulse is for him to think that he should start developing some sort of intricate way of holding the ball. In the many years I've been involved in the game I've seen some pretty weird ways of holding the ball, but it always boils down to the fact that the simplest way of throwing the ball is the best. I'd say that positioning of the wrist should be shunted aside this early in our lessons. Concentrate on facets of the game that are critical—and that brings us back to basics.

Assuming that your approach and footwork are becoming second nature, it's the armswing that you should concentrate on next. And all you have to worry about here is keeping your swing as close to your body as you possibly can.

The way to good bowling is made easier if you reduce all possibilities of making an error. Since you want to throw the ball at a fixed target, try to keep your "guns" as stationary as possible. Don't forget—you're always trying to walk straight toward your target, and when you hit that foul line you want your shoulders facing the target area. It will almost always follow that if your footwork was perfect and your shoulders were positioned correctly, your hips will be in the right position, too.

Your swing should follow the movements of your body, and there should be a minimal amount of muscle called into play. You've heard bowling-wise people say that strength doesn't play an important part in the game. Believe them—and me

—the less muscle you use, the better off you will be. Let your armswing follow the momentum your body motion gives your arm and it will never fail you. Putting your bowling hand and arm straight out and straight back and keeping it close to your hip—and trying not to waver—will get the job done.

I'll have more to tell you later on how to release the ball and make it do things for you, but for now content yourself with just learning to keep that elbow in close and your pushaway on a straight line, making sure it stays that way as your arm goes back and up and then back again.

And because the purpose of this book is to teach you how to get your game out of the doldrums and into focus, I don't intend to dwell for long on such topics as scoring and courtesy on the lanes and information of that sort. If you have purchased this book, or a friend has lent it to you, you either know how to score and what to do or you'll soon find out.

The only thing you have to know about scoring is that each time you get a spare you get ten pins plus what you knock down on the very next ball. And if you get a strike you get ten pins plus what you knock down on the next two shots—which is all I'm going to state on the subject of scoring.

As for courtesy on the lanes, well, once again all I am going to say is what I've been harping on since the beginning. Use common sense at all times and show consideration for yourself and your teammate or opponent. If you think that what you are about to do might be wrong, odds are that it is. If you're not sure about something, ask someone who is a higher-average bowler than you are and it's a cinch he'll counsel you properly. The only way you'll learn the right thing is to ask and then put what you've been told into practice.

Footwork and Armswing... Release

ALL OF THE FACTORS of good bowling are, of course, interrelated. Just as in any other sport, being proficient in one phase will not suffice. A great release and great "stuff" on the ball will do the job occasionally, but the whole picture must be filled in for the bowler to get the job done more than a reasonable number of times. You're on the approach, getting ready to deliver the shot, and that takes longer than it takes for the ball to get to the pins and do its job. What happens behind the line is more important than what hap-

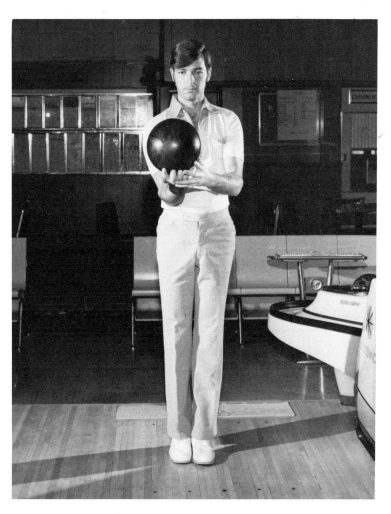

At the outset the ball is held toward the right side, with an equal share of the weight on each arm.

pens at any other stage. Do the right thing on the approach and more often than not you'll see those pins falling the way you want them to.

Okay. You've picked your ball up and you're ready to go. It's only logical that you ask, "Where should I hold the ball and how should I hold it?" To this I can only answer that you must find the height that feels most comfortable. You've seen bowlers hold the ball eye high, and you've seen others allow the ball to dangle almost at arm's length. Either method is successful, and each is used by a bowler who, because of strength or dexterity or size of his hips, was forced to hold the ball in a fashion peculiar to him. What you must do is make sure you have given equal shares of the weight of the ball to both arms by holding the ball in two hands. If you hold the ball in your right hand only, or mainly, you'll only tighten up your biceps and shoulder. By the same token, if you hold the ball directly in front of you at some stage of your delivery you're going to have to swing the ball to the side so it can pass your hip on the forward thrust.

Some bowlers circumvent this step by hefting the ball on the right side at the outset—which is the way I suggest you do it. Hold the ball toward your right side, so when you push away and then

The first step is the most important. Take a normal stride, and at the same time push the ball away from your body with both hands.

allow the arm to go behind you everything will be in a straight line. The essence of a good shot, the sure way of getting everything together, is straight swing, straight hips, and straight shoulder. As for myself, you may have noticed that when I go into my steps I always drift ever so slightly to the left. Because of that quirk, which I'm certainly not going to try and change now, I feel I must compensate by holding the ball a couple of inches "inside" my left hip. Once I go into my little weave I come right out of it because my bowling arm hasn't flown too far to the right to get me into trouble. When I do let the ball fly my arm is straight as it can be.

As for the number of steps you should take from stance to delivery, it pretty much goes without saying that four would be the right amount for the novice or intermediate bowler. We have found that the average bowler gets himself into a groove much quicker and stays that way when he doesn't tinker around with less or more steps. Many professional bowlers use a five-step approach, but they've advanced to another stage, the one in which they try to get the body into motion before they've actually started moving the ball outward from their body. Incidentally, I have known of many bowlers, built on the light side,

*As you move your left foot out for the second step, the ball should
be starting its backward swing, and should be passing your left
thigh.*

who have toyed with five steps in an effort to get a bit more momentum going. But unless you know what you're doing and will stick with it forever, don't mess around with five steps.

Four steps, naturally, will vary in distance between you and me, between someone who is six-four and someone who is five-two. To find out how far back of the foul line you should start, walk right up to the foul line and place both your heels to the line as you face the settee area. Then take four and one-half normal steps away from the line, and when you stop make a mental (or written) note on the point your feet have reached. That's where you'll be standing from now on. Repeating: four and one-half normal strides, with the half step accounting for the little slide at the end of your delivery.

Now, when you're ready to get the whole thing going, don't forget that the first step is the most important one. Take a normal stride, and at the same time push the ball away from your body with both hands, being conscious of the fact that as the second step is about to start your right hand is going to take over. As for that first step, the distance you travel with your right foot will be the same distance you'll push the ball away from you. And don't forget that when you've executed the push-

In the third stride, the ball passes your thigh and your arm is fully extended straight back.

away you must direct the ball toward the target area. Just going through the motion with no target in sight or in your mind will not do.

As you move your left foot out for the second step, the ball should be starting its backward swing, should be passing your left thigh. Now you're into it perfectly, and as you take that third stride the ball has passed your thigh, and with your arm fully extended, gone straight back but no higher than a few inches below your shoulder. Now you're all set for that crucial time when the ball is being swung, pendulum style, from way behind you. Your rhythm should see to it that as your fourth step starts the ball is almost on a line with your leg and moving at the very same speed. I've seen bowlers come to a dead stop at this point and try to make the shot without a slide. This is ruinous, and I can't emphasize that point too much. Good bowling results from a smooth slide, and you just can't get the ball going properly unless you do slide. The ball *must* be released as your left foot is sliding. Any other way and you have fouled your timing and in an effort to compensate for the imbalance you have to try and muscle the ball, pull at it to get it over the foul line reasonably close to the time that your left foot comes to a halt.

The ball must be released as your left foot is sliding.

All that remains now is for you to get the ball out over the target area. Mind you, this should not be construed as target practice. If your shoulders and body are lined up squarely to the pins, your arm, thumb, and fingers will take care of the rest. Think of it as being much the same as firing a rifle. You just don't pick up a rifle and fire. You've positioned your forearms and elbows and cocked your head to the side in preparation for the pulling of the trigger. That's how it is at point of release in bowling.

Let's backtrack now and talk about how your hand should be positioned in the ball throughout the stance, delivery, and release. Think of what you're doing as holding the ball, not gripping it. Your fingers and wrist will have a bit of work to do at the end of that slide, pushaway, backswing, and release position, and you don't want to be locked up and not have any fluidity. You should have the feeling of being able to guide the ball without ever feeling that at any moment you'll lose control. When I go out on the lanes to work out, my first thought is to get a nice, loose grip on the ball and never, ever to squeeze it. And when I'm about to let the ball go my uppermost thought is to get that lift on the ball and not just toss it on the lane.

36

I like to operate out of what I call the "V," which is a way of holding my thumb and fingers on the ball throughout the delivery and release. Normally I'll keep my thumb at a position that would approximate ten o'clock, while my other fingers would be gathered around four o'clock. When I am ready to let the ball go my thumb comes out first and then my fingers are left with the rest of the job. Naturally, with the thumb having deserted the ball, there will be an instantaneous imbalance in the weight of the ball, with the left side weighing more. My fingers thus have to take over, and in so doing they impart that lift we keep referring to. Once again I come back to this point. Regardless of where the thumb is and of what the fingers do, your armswing *must* remain straight on release. Take a fellow like Don Johnson, or the great Ned Day. They actually "figure-eighted" the ball—looped it a couple of times from push-away to delivery, but once that point of release came they went straight. The ball must have that last-step direction to give you a chance at a strike.

Each time I stand on the approach I look down at my right hand and make sure I have that V in position, and I make sure it stays that way until I let go of the ball. If I want to get more hook on a shot I still keep that V on approach and delivery,

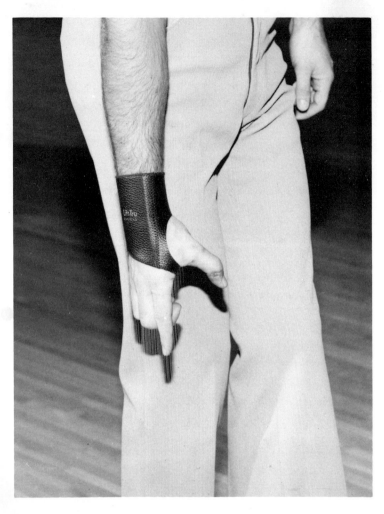

The V grip—the thumb is at a position which approximates ten

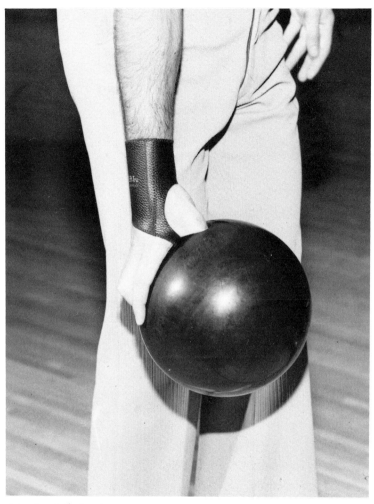

o'clock while the fingers are gathered around four o'clock.

but when I release the ball I turn my fingers almost on top of the ball once my thumb has come out. This way gives me more lift, and the result will be more hook. To give you an idea of what I mean, just visualize my thumb winding up in the six o'clock position, while my fingers are somewhere in the area of twelve o'clock. Should I want the ball to go quite straight then I just keep my thumb pointing straight up to twelve o'clock. All important is to keep your mind fixed on that V; if you start with that you won't run into too much trouble. Concentrate on your thumb's being on the left side of the ball under normal conditions and your fingers being on the right side of the ball. Then, when you're set to let it go, your fingers will take over the job of getting the lift required *after* the thumb has come out cleanly.

While I will experiment with many different hand positions as the condition dictates, if your game is not so very far advanced, you should be wary. Get your release in the same groove as you've gotten your footwork and armswing, and only then will you be equipped to toy around.

Many bowlers often have the feeling that they're "losing the ball," that they just don't have the proper feel of it. That's why you'll hear about and actually see so many of them squeezing the ball to get a stronger grip. That's bad, as is the practice used by so many bowlers of cupping the ball. By this I mean they get the ball to sort of nestle between the palm of their hand and the wrist—in a way, "mothering" it. The end result of this is for the bowler to so cut down on his fluid motion that the right kind of lift is impossible. What happens is that his wrist is actually "broken" before he lets go of the ball and the lift is lost or cut down tremendously. Keep your wrist fairly flat and cut down on the tension in your hand and almost without fail your release will be flawless and you'll get the lift you seek.

Bowlers vary in their release—that's a certainty—and the variance very often is because of physical limitations or physical superiority, and not because one bowler is doing things the right way while others are going about it all wrong. As I said, Don Johnson has that figure eight in his swing and release because he finds it gets the job done for him. Don used to be quite thin, and maybe he started to toss the ball that way because he thought he needed more turn in his hand to get stuff on the ball. Well, Don isn't so skinny any more, but who can say that what he did—and is still doing—isn't just right for him?

On the other hand, you take a bowler like Curt

When the ball is released, the thumb comes out first and

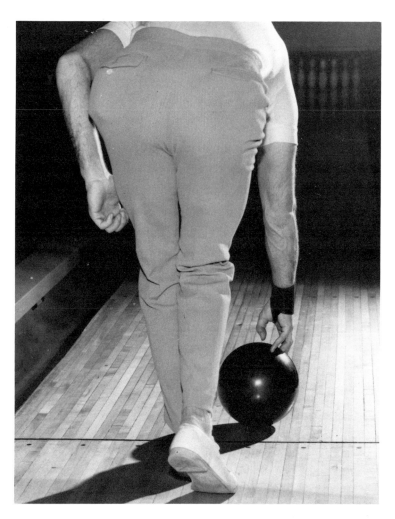

the fingers are left to impart the lift.

Schmidt, who gets hardly any hook at all. Curt worked a long time on that kind of game, feeling that the less hook he put into his shot the less margin of error there was. Well, there are two schools on that kind of strategy. One of them is that he is quite right; the other is that because he tosses a relatively straight ball he isn't getting as many revolutions on the ball as he should have. Once again I dredge up these words: accuracy, and not ball motion, might be the most important part of the game. As for Schmidt, I would say that he's doing the job more with accuracy than oomph.

If you get the chance to watch me, or fellows like Johnson or Dave Soutar, bowl, you'll notice that once we've planted our feet on the approach we take a look down at the ball. There's a method to this, too. Let me tell you about it—and let me advise you to get into the habit of doing it.

When I push the ball away from my body I want it to go in the direction of the target I'm aiming for out on the lane, and that means it's following my eyesight. If you don't push it away in that manner you'll run into trouble. If the ball should follow a line outside your target then you'll be pulling it at the last second to steer it on a true course. If you push it away inside of your target, you'll probably find that the ball will wind up somewhere behind your rump and you'll only have to compensate later on in your swing. That last-second glance at the ball to make sure it is lined up with the "sweet spot" on the lane will often eliminate any problems.

Having your bowling hand lined up is in keeping with the whole picture I have tried to outline. Your body and feet and arm must be coordinated in order to bowl well. If you deviate even slightly in any one phase you're likely to be shortchanging yourself. Don't forget that you're lugging a sixteen-pound ball up to the line, lifting it, pushing it away, swinging it back, then propelling it in a forward direction. That's a sizable load, and in order to be able to tote that load you must channel everything you have in the right direction.

Getting Involved

IN A LIFETIME of bowling you're going to spend very many dollars for league and open bowling—not counting all those tournaments and special events you'll soon be entering. Next to the expense involved in going bowling, the biggest outlay of money will go toward getting your own bowling ball.

Even coming from a bowling family, I can remember the thrill I experienced when I got my first, my very own ball. At the outset just the fact of ownership is exciting, but then the real importance of owning one's own ball becomes obvious. The ball that has been drilled out for you is just like a glove. When you slip your fingers into a custom-drilled ball you can sense almost immediately the difference between your own and the ball you "thought" fit so well at the local bowling center. What at one time you thought was a perfect fit would feel rather imperfect, compared with your own.

And that's why, almost instantly, you'll start bowling better. How your fingers go into the ball and how deep the holes are drilled and how wide the span is are all critical in the game, and you just can't bowl your best until you get your own ball. Save your pennies and dollars, and as soon as you begin knowing what the game is all about get your own. And, don't look for a bargain, insofar as getting yourself measured is concerned. Pick out the pro shop that has the very best reputation and the fellow the better bowlers go to and have him do the job for you. The difference between a bargain and an extremely competent job could be the difference in your game's showing a drastic upturn or staying the way it is.

Beyond the ball and shoes, the item that seems most intriguing to bowlers is the glove. There are several varieties, and even though some enjoy more popularity than others, the ultimate decision has to come from the bowler. All of them—at

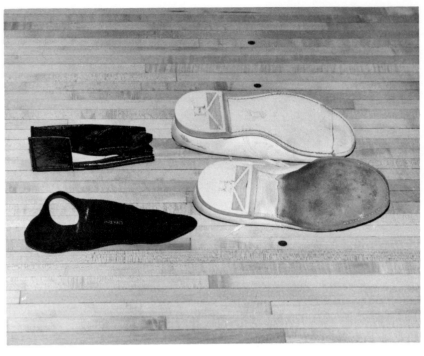

Bowling shoes, glove, and wrist support.

least all of them that I know of—are designed with one specific purpose in mind, and that is to make the ball feel lighter in the bowler's hand. Maybe it does and maybe it doesn't.

There's a "feel" to bowling that some bowlers have and never have to develop, while others are constantly trying to achieve it. I suppose if you conform to a normal pattern you might have a desire to wear one of the gloves to help you get that feel. As for me, I have worn a glove, but I don't know that my game would suffer if I didn't wear one. Bowling as many games as I do, it's a foregone conclusion that my "feel" is going to be more pronounced than the feel of a bowler who doesn't get out on the lanes as much.

If you pinned me down right here and now and asked me whether I think a bowler should get a glove, I would say yes. All of them—at least the kind we're talking about that are for the palm— serve the purpose of filling out that space between ball and hand. It will make you feel as though the ball is resting squarely in your palm, and maybe it will help you. Give it a try, but don't become a slave to the glove, as so many bowlers are. If that should happen and one night you forget the glove as you prepare for a session of league bowling, your game could be destroyed by your mind.

49

As for brand names, the two most prominent ones are the Don Carter glove and the Don Johnson Gold Palm. I'm certain there are others, but the names of these two pop into mind.

Just as there are coverings for the palm, so are there devices, if I can call them that, for the wrist. There are some bowlers who, in an effort to get "stuff" on the ball, will cock the wrist and go into some kind of distorted delivery. That's a fault that must be corrected, and one of the ways to get out of the habit is to don a device like the Dick Weber Wrist-Master or the Billy Welu Lift-Tru. This kind of glove will prevent the bowler from cocking his wrist, or he'll be aware that he is if he does, and this may help his game. I guess I just learned the right way from the very beginning— I've never had a need for either one of those aids.

My teacher—my father—never let a bad habit develop in me, and that's my advice to you. Try to nip bad habits in the bud. If something unusual ever showed itself in my game, my father would jump on it immediately, and even if it took a couple of hours he'd get me out of the habit. Some of the best bowlers in the world today could be even better if they could shake bad habits and if they had as good an instructor to go to as I did. Take a baseball player like Stan Musial. A great hitter, of course, but when he was in the batting cage he couldn't always tell if he was starting to do something wrong. It very often took someone standing outside and observing to get him into the groove once again.

After so many years out on the tour, and with the unmatchable instruction I received, I honestly feel I know as much, if not more, about the game of bowling and the conditions we face today than anyone else in the world. I don't mean to exclude the someone or someones who have made a physical and mathematical study of the game. There probably are people who know every last detail about bowling, but only on paper. I like to think that anything I say can be put into practice, and will help someone with some part of the game. I know what makes pins fall down and I know why physically, not mathematically, although by the time we're done there'll be a little addition and a little subtraction, and if I may take it a bit further, maybe even a little multiplication in your scores.

I want to get back briefly to the "stiff wrist" part of bowling, because I don't want to be so arbitrary in some things I say as to shut out all others. There are two schools of thought with respect to how the wrist should perform. One of them is to keep it rigid, while the other says that it should only be firm. My feeling is that the wrist should be rather firm until the point of release. Much of my schooling, keep in mind, came from old-timers—men like my dad and Andy Varipapa and Ned Day. They had to be "wrist bowlers" because they had some pretty tough pins to knock down. They realized that the strength of a bowler in getting that "lift" came more from the wrist than the fingers.

Try holding an object out in front of you and lifting it with your fingers only. Pretty tough. But if you get a little wrist into the effort it becomes much easier. That's the way it is with your ball at the point of release. The fingers will help impart the revolutions, but the message comes from the wrist. Ask me what I am and I'll come right out and say that I'm a wrist bowler—always have been and probably always will be.

The way I see it, if there's some tenseness to the wrist, there has to be the same tenseness in the fingers. I've heard bowlers of every caliber and from all parts of the country using the expression "getting fingers on the ball." Well, they can call it what they will, but the way I bowl—with the accent on a firm wrist—it means "getting wrist on the ball."

There's something else about the way I'm built

that should indicate to anyone who has seen me bowl that I'm doing an awful lot with my right hand. I first began to notice it a year or two after I really began to put everything into bowling— my right bicep and forearm were getting bigger. I never got alarmed about it; I just took it for granted that an overdeveloped arm was the result of doing the same thing over and over with it. I've seen carpenters who hammer and saw constantly get to be the same way, and I've also seen the same overdevelopment in just about every baseball pitcher. It has absolutely nothing to do with strength, and I can state that even though I used to go in for weight lifting—and sometimes still do. Bowling doesn't make many demands on your strength—and the fact that many women can toss the ball as hard as I do ought to prove that there's no accent on muscle in the game. Maybe it's all that "wrist" I'm getting into each and every shot I make.

I would like to make some comments on my weight lifting—on anyone's weight lifting. At no time do I tell myself that I'm doing it because I want to get strong, which is the way it is with many young adults. I'm not trying to get strong; it's just that, since the pressure can build up when you're bowling out on the tour and since the game makes so many demands on the legs as well, I believe it's a good thing to keep in topnotch physical condition. I don't know if any of you out there will ever turn professional, but if you do you'll know what I mean. When you get nervous—and it need not be while bowling—the place you'll feel it first and most, and the place where it'll be most evident, will be in your legs. They're not kidding about wobbly knees in pressure situations. I know —I've been there a few times, though not recently and not too noticeably.

While I concentrate very much on building up my legs through special exercises, I also do a job on myself upstairs—in my mind. I believe that I have won most of the battle when I can control my emotions and when I feel I can make my body do what I want it to do. There has never been a man who didn't experience some fear, some uneasiness about the unknown. Well, I try to anticipate what's going to happen and prepare myself for it in every way.

That accounts, I suppose, for my feeling in much better mental and physical shape before the winter tour than before our summer schedule. I don't fool myself; I know that the big money is usually in those tournaments whose finals are shown over national television. When I feel that

I'm on the brink of a clutch situation in which I have to do my best, I'm prepared for that contingency. If I allow myself to think of the tremendous pressure, if I allow myself to think that I may not rise to the occasion, I'm failing myself and anyone who may be rooting for me.

In Milwaukee early in 1972—at the Miller High Life Open—they wired me and a few other pro bowlers to test our reaction under emotional stress. A team of doctors from Wisconsin University at LaCrosse came to the lanes for a few days; they attached little transmitters to our chests to record how we performed on first shots (the strike ball) and on spares, and to see what emotions we felt when we were on a string of strikes that kept going—or broke off.

They had me hooked up on the night before the TV finals. Many people in the audience asked me if it didn't bother me, having that little transmitter sending out signals to the unit behind the lanes. Honestly, it didn't. I don't know exactly what findings they came up with, but I'd certainly be overly modest if I didn't say that even though there was so much riding on my performance that night I felt cool and confident. However, the men who were monitoring the machine when I shot a 300 game said there was quite a bit of movement on that chart when it came down to the final shots. Analyze it as you will. I feel that my physical condition and constant practice prepared me for that situation and has me "combat ready" at all times.

Okay—let's move on. You know about the ball to use and the glove to wear and what your mental and physical approach to the game should be. It's time now to discuss the very serious business of knocking down pins. And for this I can't impress on you too much the importance of seeking out an instructor.

If your average is below the 190 mark—I mean, if you're not competing in the better leagues and you're not a professional—you should find someone to tutor you. There are countless good teachers around, but make sure you find one who is extremely confident about his own game. Only then will confidence be imparted to you. Almost every bowling establishment, in just about every city, will have one or more tutors more than willing to help you with your game. Don't forget— the proprietor of that bowling establishment wants you to bowl better as much as you want to. He wants you as a customer, and you'll be one only if your game shows an upturn or if you stay at a peak level.

Whether you are learning at the feet of someone else, or doing it by yourself, the next thing you want to learn is to spot-bowl. By that I mean picking out an area on the lane you want your ball to cross. You've probably also heard that you should never spot-bowl until your average gets to be quite high and that you should sight only the pin area early in your development. Wrong. The only way you're going to learn how to be accurate is to get your eye trained on a board or two out there close to the foul line.

Starting out, you should attempt to get every ball you roll to cross the second arrow, and you know what that means. There are thirty-nine boards, each about one inch wide, on just about every lane. Every fifth board is darker in color. You can call these boards "arrows" or "markers" or "range finders." But call them what you will, just bear in mind that your target at the beginning is that second arrow, meaning you should be trying to get the ball to roll over the tenth board from the right. By starting out at this point, you'll soon develop the versatility that's needed to make an adjustment in your game. Because for sure—there'll be many, many adjustments in the games and years to come because the characteristics of lanes change from lane to lane as well as from house to house in city to city.

Once you've gotten a bead on that second arrow, don't make the mistake of thinking you have a mind's-eye picture and that your eye can rove. Many bowlers begin to think they can look at their spot, stop looking as they take their four-step approach, then come back to it at the last moment. That's a mistake. No peeking allowed. Don't assume that the ball has gone over the arrow or that it missed. Keep looking and you'll know for sure. Your head should stay down and your arm should reach out for the target, not toward the lane to the right or the one on the left.

I'll let you in on a little trick I teach all my pupils. I tell them that they're not to look up from their spot until they sense that the ball is about to hit the pins. This will become instinctive in you, as it does in everyone. It takes only a few seconds for the ball to travel those sixty feet, so it really isn't too much of an investment of time if you make absolutely sure the ball has hit the target area.

There are even many pros out on the tour who "cut their shot short." They think all they have to do is put some fingers into the ball to get a strike. Well, they'll get some, of course, but my way is to try and execute every shot to perfection. You must

58

follow through on each ball and you must get a bead on that spot. I'm rather friendly with Barry Asher, another pro on the tour and a darn good bowler. But Barry will stray from the object on occasion, and I have to drum the basics into him —head down, follow through, and don't neglect to do either even if you feel that the release was less than perfect.

There are bowlers who instruct their pupils on all levels to do something else once the ball has reached the pins. They tell the students to follow the path of the ball through the pins and see where it falls off into the pit end. I don't subscribe to this at all. First of all, you can't really be that exact in telling where the drop-off point is. The difference between a strike and a split can be only an inch or so, and the area from pin deck to pit end is so far away from your eyes that you'll never be able to learn much. This is complicated by the fact that the ball can deflect in many different ways once it has hit a pin. Besides, you'll probably learn your lessons so well on how to get strikes and spares that you won't have much reason to suspect that you didn't do marvelously on almost every shot.

Very early in your game you will either detect a difference in the condition of each lane upon which you bowl or you will want to know how to tell if there *is* a difference. As you have heard here and elsewhere, each and every lane at each and every bowling center is treated with oil conditioner on a regular basis. By regular I mean daily—or at least it should be that way.

With countless games bowled each day, if measures were not taken to protect the wood on which the ball rolls friction would soon destroy the lane. So a coating of oil is applied to each lane, and the distribution of that oil, its consistency, how far out it is applied and to what width it is put down, all are important to your game. It goes without saying that the heavier the oil, the more your ball will slide before going into a roll. You should be able to distinguish between lanes that are heavy with oil and those that are drier.

Until the bowler is able to come up with a repetitious shot, one in which his release is just about the same all the time, he is not really going to be able to tell just how a lane is. Unless the lane is in an extreme condition, it will take much time before you will be knowledgeable enough to change your shot to fit a particular condition.

You will hear good bowlers talk about lanes being two or three or one or four boards different from the way they were the day before. Or words to that effect. What they mean is that, playing their usual angle and with their usual release, the ball is reacting in a different fashion. If the lanes are slick, the bowler no doubt will change his angle to be certain that his ball makes it to the pocket area. If the lanes are dry, he will probably have to compensate by moving to his left and allowing his shot to cross over more boards on its way to the pocket. Remember, though, that it is quite hard for the amateur or sometime bowler to be able to make a true determination, because usually he doesn't have the correct amount of roll on his ball to be certain how it will react.

You'll notice how I keep stressing the fact that, until you get your game into a groove where you toss the ball the same way each time, it will be almost impossible to be able to "read" lanes properly. The bowler who is averaging in the area of 160 will not be able to make the called-for adjustment, even if he is able to tell how the lanes are, because he will not be able to duplicate his shot each and every time.

I have been asked by many bowlers to give my opinion on what an "ideal" condition would be. It's impossible to give an answer to that because everyone tosses the ball in a different way. Better bowlers will almost always prefer a "tight" condition, one in which there is a bit more oil on the lane than usual. Of course, pros don't call them "tight"—we like to call them "right." Anytime we have a condition in which we don't have to be concerned with crossing very many boards, or to try and work up a big hook, we are better off. Too many lower-average bowlers still think that the roundhouse curve will knock down the most pins. About all the wide sweeping curve will get you these days is a lot of spares to shoot at.

This might be the best time to describe in some detail the dimensions of the lane on which you are bowling. It may be that you have heard or seen information to the contrary, but all you should have to know about a lane is that those boards we keep talking about are just a fraction wider than one inch. There are thirty-nine boards to each lane, and the lane is always forty-two inches wide.

The area where your ball initially hits the lane is the place where the wood is hardest, because that's the part of the lane that takes the most punishment. So, from the foul line to the area just about where you see the range finders, the wood is maple. From that point on—and the difference is visible—the wood is pine, because your ball will now be going into a different phase. Pine is softer than maple and allows for greater ball action where it is needed. Then the kind of wood used reverts to maple, because the ball is now ready for the final crash into the pins, and this is a part of the lane that is taking punishment once again. All in all, there is a distance of sixty feet from foul line to the one pin, give or take half an inch, and to complete the picture there is a minimum of fifteen feet to the approach. Put both figures together and you have an area that is longer than the distance from home plate to the pitcher's mound in baseball.

Those one-inch-wide strips of wood—the boards —are actually nailed together, but not in the fashion you think. The nails are driven in sideways to prevent the boards from popping up. The whole construction is called "tongue and groove," which is a term widely used in the furniture industry. There are occasions when one or more of those boards do pop up. When they do they can wreck your game, because the ball will be kept from following a true path. When a board does rise the fault can almost always be traced to the fact that the wood was "green" when it was installed. It takes a couple of years for the strips of wood to settle into the alley bed, and they don't always settle in the same manner.

If your ball does hit one of those high boards, it will be thrown off to the right or left. I don't want to mislead you, however. The high board or boards I speak of are practically invisible. You can't see them and you can't hear them. On my shot I can tell almost instantly if I've hit a high board—and I can also tell from what direction I've hit it. If I hit a high board on the right it would straighten out my shot. If I went directly over it it would kill the roll. And if I caught the high board on the left it would probably send my shot to the left of the head pin.

I tell you all these things just to increase your knowledge of bowling and not because I am trying to instill in you fear of the game and your shot. Once you graduate to the high-average class you are going to have a burning desire to keep further-ing your education. Boards, high or low or what have you, are just one of the many facets of this game of ours, and the more familiar you are with the pitfalls and terminology of the sport the better you will be in the long run.

At the beginning of your bowling career, and right on through the very last ball you toss, upper-most in your mind should be the fact that those pins at the other end of the lane are your enemies. But in order to be a more complete bowler, you should know something about the pins—what they're made of and what they do when they're hit.

The standard pin today is scientifically produced under quite rigid specifications. There are usually seven layers of wood assembled with various adhesives, and then the layers of wood are encased in a sock made of nylon. Then the entire pin is covered with a plastic shell.

The nylon sock over the wood is something not too many bowlers know of. It is, to all intents and purposes, just what I say it is—a sock—made of pure nylon and with a stretch quality to it. Its purpose is to fill in some of the air space that was prevalent in pins some years ago. Because of that air space, which seemed to be unavoidable, pins would often crack and chip. The manufacturers found that the sock made the pin more stable and gave it longer life. The constant pounding of the ball against the pin used to beat the wood over its entire surface and cause the wood to "fall away" from the plastic. That doesn't seem to happen any more with the nylon covering between wood and plastic. Putting it another way, when the ball hits the pin now, it forces the plastic to fall against the nylon and the nylon, giving an adhesion to all the different materials, in turn molds itself to the wood.

At the core of the pin there is nothing. That's right—nothing. This is called the "void," and it is something that has come to pass only in recent years, when the weight of the average pin has come down from three pounds eight or nine ounces to our current three pounds five or six ounces. There are pins that even go way down to three-two, but you don't see too many of them around. I'd say that most bowling centers use wood that's in the three-five, three-six, or three-seven class, but many places will use much lighter wood, and there's a reason behind that.

There isn't a bowling proprietor around—and don't forget I speak as one—who doesn't want his bowlers to come up with high scores. And, if he can get his bowlers high scores and not do anything illegal, why shouldn't he? Lighter pins will definitely make for bigger scores, and even in our place we'll often have three-twos and three-threes. But the proprietor pays a price for this, because the lighter set of pins will not have the durability of heavier pins. New pins and the servicing and refurbishing of old ones make up a sizable part of the proprietor's expenditures each season.

The way we take care of our pins—and I don't think we have to go into the care of the bowling pin here—we will get about four or five thousand lines (games) out of a set of pins when we use three-twos. When we use three-six and three-seven pins oftentimes we'll get six or seven thousand lines out of them. That means quite a bit of savings, but you have to weigh scoring against long life of the pin and make your own determinations. Giving your bowlers a fair and fine scoring condition can mean so much added revenue to the proprietor that it could swing the balance toward the lighter pin.

There was a time when allowable wood was as light as two pounds fourteen ounces and went way up to about four pounds. Most houses now will use three-twos as the minimum, but there is a restriction put on the variance of weights in a set. In order to speed up play most places will keep twenty or twenty-one pins in the machines. This way there is very little delay as the machine sets a new rack, while other pins are in readiness. The rules state that all pins must be within three ounces of each other to be "legal," but frankly I don't know if that rule is adhered to in all bowling centers.

I have heard quite a few bowlers say that they can tell the weight of the pins that are on the deck by the way they react when the ball hits. Well, I defy anyone to tell with any degree of consistency. The kind of condition on the lane you're bowling on will often have an effect on the way the pins splatter—or don't. It's possible that the ball will not grab the lane as it heads toward the pocket, or it's possible that the angle you're forced to play is not the one you want, and when you do something you're not accustomed to doing it could change your analysis about what's happening at the pit end of the lane.

I have seen bowlers alter their angle of attack —adjusting even though they didn't want to—and they soon find that even though the pins may have been three-twos they "carried tough." Then, too, I've seen houses with extremely clean bowling surfaces on which the ball took a true roll and knocked pins down like they were pick-up sticks, even though the pins were on the heavy side.

On the tour we usually bowl against pins in the three-five to three-seven class. I would venture a guess that most of the fellows on the pro tour don't care what the weight of the pin is. Most of them throw such strong balls that they are more concerned with reading the lane and coming up with a smooth delivery than whether the pins will fall properly. To draw another analogy with golf, you don't have to give every shot your all-out effort to do the right thing. If a golfer comes up to a 175-yard hole he's going to take out a three-iron. If he's teeing up for a par-five, 550-yarder he's going to get out that number-one wood because he needs his best effort. If the pins are on the light side, the bowler knows he doesn't have to "bomb" them. If they're heavy, he doesn't want to trickle the ball down the lane. Just playing his best shot in a true fasion will do the job.

In bowling centers where there are "sweepers" going on, or in tournaments where the proprietor wants to keep scoring on the low side, it's almost a certainty that he will put heavier wood in the machines.

There was a sweeper some time ago in Saint Louis in which a lot of money was at stake. I don't know where the man who was running the show got them, but he had pins that weighed almost four and half pounds in the racks. The tournament was not an approved (sanctioned) one, so anything went. A few fellows I know of went out and got themselves a twenty-pound bowling ball to do the job—the maximum weight allowed in legitimate bowling competition is sixteen pounds—and it sure did, because they won the top three money spots. What those fellows did was to drill out holes in the ball—one on top and one on bottom—and they just filled the holes with lead—a few pounds of it. By putting holes top and bottom they still managed to provide the ball with a true balance, but what they did is illegal in bowling competition.

I'd like to say here that I've heard of a few—not too many—fellows who have come out on the tour and experimented with balls that were lighter than the allowable sixteen pounds. Almost without fail they either went back to full-weighted balls or went back home to try another sport. At best, the war between ball and pins is an unfair one. The pins win out too many times. Why give the pins an added advantage by using a lighter ball? The heavier the ball, the stronger it will hit. All you have to do is provide the accuracy.

I think this would be the right time to delve into the ball itself—to discuss what it is made of, and without getting too technical, how it is made.

Though there have been bowling balls made of other substances, just about all of the ones in use today are made of either hard rubber or plastic. The plastic ball, for reasons we'll get into later on, has become quite popular in recent years because of the showings of some bowlers, and all manufacturers of note are now putting out balls made of both.

There's no quarreling with one factor: the less expensive the ball, the more likely it is that cheaper products are used in its manufacture. At the center of all bowling balls is the core. In the less expensive ball almost anything available will do—cork or pieces of scrap rubber. And when the ball is plastic it doesn't have the density of rubber, so the core is enlarged. The well-made rubber ball, the one that sells for thirty dollars and upwards, is usually the best. That's not to say it gets the best results for everyone, just that the best materials go into its making.

After the core is established—its thickness and its composition—layer upon layer of rubber or plastic is applied to the sphere. Then the most important step is taken—application of the shell, which is about one inch in thickness. This outer cover—the overcoat, so to speak—is made of high-quality rubber and in two pieces, which are fitted over the core and layers. The two pieces then are vulcanized (fused) through high pressure, a force so tremendous that you can't tell where the joining was made. With the plastic ball, where vulcanization as we know it is not feasible, you can tell where the two shells come together, because the plastic is clear and you can almost see into the ball.

I have simplified the construction of the ball only because at this point I want to discuss something that is much more relative to your game, and for the sake of clarity I didn't want to get into the subject until I gave you the basics. I am referring to the "weight block" that goes into each and every ball manufactured and has gone into millions upon millions of bowling balls in years past.

Not very far underneath the outer surface of the ball a material of much higher density than even the outer shell is placed. The weight block comes in assorted sizes and shapes, but the actual weight is usually about four ounces. The shape can be four inches by four inches, or even two by four, depending on who the manufacturer is. Some even make the block in pancake form. A most interesting procedure is then followed to determine exactly where the center of that weight block is.

In order to know which part of the ball is now the heaviest, the ball is immersed in a tub of mercury; the portion that contains the weight block will rise to the top of the "bath." A mark is made on the ball to show the exact center, for use when the finger holes are drilled out, and then the name of the manufacturer is stamped on. This is a critical stage because, as you will see a bit later, the weight block has a great deal to do with some rather interesting and intricate maneuvers a bowler can execute in an effort to get his bowling ball to do different things out on different lanes.

So far we have gone into many of the factors involved in learning both to be a good bowler and to sound like one, but there is one significant point we haven't touched upon, one whose drastic effect on one's shot and the lanes underfoot was overlooked for too long. It is, however, a topic that we are getting to learn more and more about as we delve into all the variables of bowling. What I'm referring to is weather, and by that I mean humidity.

So many key issues have been raised in recent years that it is almost impossible to believe that this subject was not raised and explored much more thoroughly in recent years. There seems little doubt now, certainly after what we have learned in lengthy seminars held with experts representing the Professional Bowlers Association, the American Bowling Congress, and the Bowling Proprietors Association of America, that atmospheric conditions often will determine how well or poorly a given bowler will do.

Moisture on the hand of the bowler is almost incidental when you think of the various effects humidity can have. First of all, a humid condition can wreck a bowler's game on the approach because, as you know, a smooth, uninterrupted slide

73

is vital. Then, too, the bowling pin itself will absorb moisture, making it a bit harder to topple. But perhaps the worst effect humidity can have is the way it will affect the lane, because that protective coating of oil will react differently depending on what the humidity index is. Many bowlers will make radical adjustments in their game when they know the city or the house they're in is near a large body of water, or if there has been a prolonged dry or wet spell.

It would be perfect, naturally, if someone could come up with an ideal atmospheric condition in all bowling centers and see to it that the temperature and humidity index is kept constant. But that's virtually impossible, especially at some of the professional tournaments, where great crowds of people will gather at a house to watch the bowlers in action.

Remember, as you progress in your game, that the weather, in and out of the place you're bowling in, can and will have an effect on your scoring. You won't be able to do anything about the weather, but you will be able to take the necessary steps to keep your game on an even keel.

Just a few more bits of preliminary information here and then we'll move on to other facets of the game. And while some of the points we will touch on may seem somewhat trivial, not being faithful to each and every one of them could betray you in a situation that could be embarrassing or costly. The pros take these items quite seriously, so why shouldn't you—and all the other members of your team?

Once you pick up your bowling ball from the rack or the turntable and step onto the approach, it's you against the pins. The fellow behind you or the one on either side cannot help you; he can only be a hindrance. If you don't heckle someone who's about to go into his shot, you'll never be heckled yourself. But what is most important for you is that you must almost "psych" yourself once you've hoisted the ball into position and taken your stance. It works for me and I know it works for every one of the topnotch bowlers—concentrate on what you are about to do and you'll be a much better bowler. There are several better bowlers who will go on record as having built their game with equal doses of skill and concentration. If you can get up to the lane, ready yourself for your shot, and be oblivious to the fellow who's a few lanes away, you've added pins to your average.

Unless you're up in the range of bowling forty or fifty games a week, you're not likely to be bothered with swollen or callused or even bruised fingers—unless, of course, you have an ill-fitting ball. But you must consider the possibility and you must know what to do about it. I have always experienced some difficulty with my bowling thumb, and I suppose I always will. Some bowlers never are distressed or bothered at all, while with others it's chronic. In fact, in a tournament not very long ago where I was up among the leaders, and where I thought I had a great shot at the championship, I had to withdraw after I tore some of the skin from my thumb on a succession of shots. I tried three or four remedies, but none of them worked and I had to quit.

If you develop a callus on your fingers and thumb it could work both ways—be of benefit to you to help you withstand bruises or be a problem if one of them should tear away. There are an armful of preparations on sale at all bowling alleys to toughen the skin or make it more pliable, to protect the skin or to allow a certain amount of pressure to seep through to help you build callus. None of them will be harmful and most of them work. Just don't become a slave to any of the gloves or solutions or patches or whatnot. Good bowling comes from the head and the feet and the arm, not from a patent medicine or a gimmick. If something happens make use of a remedy; don't try things just for the sake of trying them.

And to wrap up this segment of the book—the one that has given you a few of the rudiments and some of the ins and outs—just one final word of advice. This pertains to repetition—the right kind as opposed to the wrong kind.

The secret of good sport, of being a little better than ordinary, lies with doing the right thing all the time—or at least attempting to do the right thing all the time. If you can repeat your arm-swing and your legwork and make your mind go along with it you're ahead of the game, providing you're doing everything properly. However, your game will come apart at the seams if you insist on doing something, even though you've been told by most people what you're doing is wrong.

The longer you repeat poor moves, the longer it will take you to come out of it. It's like biting your nails or overeating. If you fall into bad habits they become second nature, and you'll find that there's an inner resistance to breaking such habits. If it's pointed out to you by someone competent, or if the printed word indicates that you're doing something to hurt your game, you'd better believe it. It almost goes without saying that if you look like you're bowling well, the odds are that you *are* bowling well. The fellow with the perfect form

77

likely will be the better bowler, or at least have the bedrock on which to improve his game. If you're told that seven steps on your delivery are too much, take that someone's word for it. If you're told your backswing is too high, it is. If a buddy observes that you are rushing the line, then you are. And you should set about changing things around. That's why you're reading this book, isn't it?

The Strike

IT'S AN ACKNOWLEDGED fact that getting
to the pocket can be tricky—complicated, if you
prefer. The weapon may vary in size and color
and the route you take will often be tortuous.
But the object is about as simple as it possibly
could be. The ultimate on any given shot is the
strike, and the ultimate insofar as your game
score goes is to get twelve of them in a row. Any
time you knock down less than ten pins on your
first shot in a frame you have not accomplished
what you set out to do. It may appear that you
tossed the ball perfectly, it may look as though
the ball hit the pocket perfectly, and it may seem
that there wasn't a hint of a mistake between your
first step and release, but when you don't get a

strike you have done something wrong or something went wrong with the ball as it headed toward the pins.

Naturally, all of us know what happens when we get a strike—all ten pins fall, though not necessarily in the classic style of "pow, there they go." Sometimes the pins bounce back on the lanes after hitting the sides or back and sometimes a pin wiggles before falling. What *does* happen on a classic strike ball is that the ball hits less than half the pins on the pin deck. To be specific, that sixteen-pound ball, assuming you are a right-hander, will hit the one and the three (those two pins stand guard at the pocket); then it will hit the five pin after which it will veer off and topple the nine. Actually, the three pin gets to the nine first, but the ball does hit that area.

Everything else that follows on the strike shot happens only because you set those four pins in motion in the proper fashion. The one pin hits the two, which then hits the four, which is then supposed to take out the seven. The six pin, activated by the three, then crashes into the ten. The five pin, which was hit solidly by the ball, is then supposed to complete the job by going slightly to the left and putting the eight pin in the pit.

Obviously, we aren't going to get strikes on

every effort. So what happened? Well, assuming the ball hit the pocket, it means some pin or pins didn't do their job. For instance, the four may have jumped over the seven, or it may have gone too far to the left. The same may have been true with the six as it failed in its mission to fell the ten. If the five was hit improperly, no doubt it went too far to the right (as you face the pins) and the result was a solid eight—meaning the eight pin remained "glued."

I don't want to generalize when speaking of the manners in which pins fall, but there are so many factors involved that sometimes we have to guess as to why this or that pin or pins stayed up. Leaving the ten on a good hit could have resulted from tossing the ball too hard. It may also be that the pin-setting machine may have dropped the ten— or any other pin for that matter—off spot. Remember, you are tossing a round object at a target that is also rounded, and that makes for some rather risky chain reactions. You can't expect the pins to do the same thing every time. You can only hope they will.

We should pay some attention to just what the different kinds of strikes are. Suppose we start with the "swish," because that's the one that always occurs when we haven't really put the ball smack in the pocket. Because you haven't hit the pocket solidly, the five pin is driven to its right and into the eight and then glances over to take out the seven.

Through the years I have been asked by many people whether on some lanes, under some conditions, I might deliberately try to get a "swishing" strike, instead of "burying" the ball in the pocket. If you're going to stay on the same pair of lanes for a good many games, you should only attempt to hit the pocket solidly. If you're making a mistake—and most of the mistakes the good bowlers make is to the left of the head pin—then you would try to adjust for a lighter hit. On the pro tour, where you are constantly on the move, never shooting more than one game on a pair of lanes, then you take them the way they come.

Pros talk about an "area" they can play, meaning that the ball will get enough of the pocket to almost guarantee a fair number of strikes. If that's the case, they'd be wrong to try for a picture strike. The pin that will remain standing on a pocket hit that is a shade too high is the four. That's the one that plagues the pro. When I leave the four, then I make the necessary moves to get a lighter pocket hit. When the pressure gets great, that's when you'll find bowlers coming in on the nose. There's a lot of pocket on the right, so why not move your target area a half board or so?

There are times when we bowl at a house where there is a pair of lanes, or a couple pairs of lanes, that are quite easy to get lined up on. If I, or anyone for that matter, should find that the swishing strike is working on one lane, and the solid pocket hit on the other, there is absolutely no reason to make a move. The big payoff is on the pins falling down, and no one is marking your paper, giving you an A for solid and an A-minus for swish.

On the wall shot, the ball comes in even lighter on the headpin and knocks it right over to the wall on the left side. The pin then caroms back onto the lane and takes out the four, five, and seven. If there were no side wall, and the one pin just kept on going, the four, five, and seven would remain standing. It's that simple.

Though it doesn't happen frequently on an apparently perfect pocket hit, there are times when the seven or the eight is left standing. It's merely that something went wrong with the chain reaction touched off. The four pin probably was hit on a poor angle by the two and was, in turn, driven straight back, instead of taking out the seven. There is no adjustment you can make. However, when the solid ten is plaguing you, when it stands there glaring at you even though you are positive you've done the right thing, it is evident that you need correction in your loft or speed. When the ten stands up it means only that the six pin went spinning around the ten instead of into it. Hardly ever will the six go flying *over* the ten, as happens with the four and seven once in a while.

My advice to the bowler who leaves too many tens is for him to try and get the ball farther out over the foul line and not "lay it short." By that I mean imparting an almost instant roll to the ball, instead of allowing it to slide first before starting to roll. You'll remember we touched on that earlier, about the ball's going through three distinctive stages—slide, roll, and hook. If the shot loses too much in the first stage it's almost a certainty it won't do the required job.

Of course, if the bowler has to play a drastic inside line—putting the ball over the fourth (middle) arrow—it cuts down his angle of attack so much that the pins, once they are hit, cannot rattle around in the proper fashion. But if the condition is such that you must play inside, then all you can do is depend on an alteration in your loft to help you topple the ten. At best, though, this is sketchy advice. Those solid tens are a part of the game, I guess, and for every one you leave I suppose somewhere, sometime, you're getting a strike on a less-than-perfect strike ball. Just learn to live with it, and try to look at it this way. If you're hitting the pocket fairly consistently, you really won't want to tinker around with your shot because you've left a couple of ten pins—especially out on the tour, where you're never confined to shooting all your games on only one pair of lanes, as in league play. Most of the younger players on the tour never really learned to get locked in on one pair, which was the way I was taught when I was young.

There is a breed of bowler today who could pull bricks out of a wall each time he leaves the four pin on a solid hit. Evidently he feels that just because the strike shot was a mite high he still should have gotten the four. I don't feel that way, and I never have. When I've left the four it means simply that I didn't execute the shot. Some bowlers seem to have the knack of "tripping" the four, but most don't. Tripping means that, even though the pocket was hit too solidly, still the two pin managed to nick its neighbor to the rear. More loft and more speed and moving further inside should conquer the four-pin blues, if you have them. An encouraging note, too, is the fact that when you take out all pins but the four, odds are that your ball is doing a pretty good job when it gets to the pins. If it wasn't, then you'd be seeing more than a few splits down there on the high hit.

Another leave that is disturbing to the good bowler—and it's mostly good bowlers who leave this one—is the four-nine. Once again, it means that your ball has hit too high (leaving the four) and then finished so strongly that both ball and three pin failed to get the necessary time to take out the nine. Pros who leave this one seldom are as glum as when they've left the ten. If I were bowling on a "track" condition I would loft the ball a bit more and apply more speed to the shot. However, if I had determined that this wasn't a track condition, I'd merely follow the oil—a concept I'll go into in detail later—to the pocket and move in a bit deeper.

Many's the time I've tossed the ball, or seen someone else toss it, and after it had rolled just a little way I'd think to myself, "Eight-ten." It's the "pocket split" all right, because, while the ball has definitely hit the pocket, the trouble is that it lost most of its "oomph" when it got there. Mind you, I'm talking about a poor shot that results in the eight-ten, not when the pins may have been off spot. If you do leave it, and you won't come across it too often, once again it's the result of a weak

86

release or a poor angle. A good bowler who is aware at the point of release that his ball lost most of the necessary revolutions (nine is the right amount, give or take one or two)* because of a weak delivery, won't change his angle. He'll just stay at the same spot on his next strike attempt and try to get more into the shot. If he notes that the ball has slid, and not driven, into the pins, then he knows instantly he has to move farther outside with his shot or slow up his speed.

It stands to reason that someone who tosses a full roller (there aren't too many of these fellows around) will find that his ball will make far fewer revolutions because each full roll is consuming the entire circumference. For someone like myself, or any of the hundreds of others who toss a semiroller (some call it a semispinner), the ball is revolving on less of its surface, perhaps ten inches or under, so this kind of shot will provide more revolutions. Every ball starts out in a skid roll, then goes into a power roll before going into its final stage—the hook. (Even though we talk of "roll" you must keep in mind that the ball is

---

* I've come up with this figure only because pupils of mine keep pressing me for an answer. Keep in mind that a bowling ball is twenty-seven inches in circumference and there are a few different ways to toss it.

always in some kind of skid, or slide. It never fully grabs the lane, and as a matter of fact, it actually bounces along as it moves over tiny ruts and grooves and valleys.)

On almost every shot I take you will notice that the ball appears to come off my fingers rather reluctantly. I consider this part of my battle plan, getting the ball to hang on to my fingers for a split second so that I can get it farther out over the foul line than do most other bowlers. It's that extra loft I keep referring to. The lane finishes we bowl on today are much harder than they used to be, so my method is not to attempt to "belly" the ball out to the track and then try to make it come back again. It just won't do that. It won't go out three or four boards and then come back. Instead, I try to "hold the line." You must be fairly direct, but you still have to have enough lift on the shot to knock down pins.

A long time ago I discovered that the extra loft I put on my shot will delay the roll for five or six feet and thus keep the ball from hooking too early. Maybe it sounds complicated, but it's a basic part of my game. In the days of the softer finishes, you could throw the ball out, "belly" it, and still depend on it to come back and finish well. Lay a ball short these days and the ball will go into a roll and hook prematurely, and there go your chances at ringing up strikes.

If you go bowling on a regular basis, or if you watch the pros bowl, you have seen so many of the better bowlers turning to the plastic ball, forgoing the traditional rubber ball—to accomplish exactly the same thing I've been talking about, keeping the ball from going into a roll and hook too soon. The plastic ball, they say, achieves the same thing without lofting. The ball gets "through the heads" (foul line to arrows) in a slide, almost being prohibited from doing anything but sliding, thus retaining much more impact when it is needed —especially when it starts to weave its way into the pocket. You never want it to lose any of its punch.

A little while back I mentioned something about "following the oil." At this time I'd like to delve into that subject, because all good bowlers know that the way the oil (lane conditioner) is applied to the lanes has a positive or negative effect on their game. American Bowling Congress specifications at one time stressed that all lanes had to be oiled equally. This meant that gutter to gutter (left to right), oil had to be set down on each and every board. The ABC may have altered its way of thinking in recent years when it was discovered that equal oiling often led to unequal conditions. On some surfaces the left-hander had a decided advantage, while on others the right-hander had a better shot.

At any rate, the proprietor who had to comply with ABC rules as far as how wide the oiling procedure had to go, had the option of deciding how far down the lane he wanted the oil applied. Some of them would put oil down thirty or forty feet or so on a daily basis, and touch touch the back ends. The thinking was—and rightly so—that if they didn't apply oil as frequently to the last third of the lane the boards would dry out and the bowler's ball would have more hooking power once it passed the oil and went into a higher friction zone. The motive was to increase scoring by their bowlers, because that's the name of the game. Give your customers better scores and they'll give you their business year after year.

Now suppose the place you're bowling at has been resurfaced, or it does not have a pronounced track—an area where the lacquer underneath has been worn down. That means when the oil is applied it will be sitting there, equally distributed over all thirty-nine boards. But once you start bowling it stands to reason that some of that oil is going to be "pushed" to the right and left and a dry area is going to be created. (Actually, I should say there will be a "drier" area where the ball will hook more.) So if a bowler wants to minimize his chances at losing his shot, he should be aware that if he makes a mistake and his ball misses by a board it probably will come back toward the pocket, because once his ball hits the dry area it will grab more and hook more. Thus, if he follows the oil—plays into it—it will hold the line if he tossed it well, and if he didn't he gets a second chance because the ball will find its way back from the "beaten path."

Bowlers constantly ask me what is the ideal place to line up on the approach for the strike ball. Here again it's impossible to provide a formula for all lanes, for all bowlers, but of course there has to be a rule of thumb. What I generally do is place my left foot on the seventeenth board and set my gaze on the second arrow, which is the tenth board from the right. On almost all of my shots I—and most good bowlers—follow that pattern—my left foot will slide on a board that is usually six boards from the target I'm aiming for. Ideally then, the ball will "belly" one or two boards on its way to crossing the second arrow.

Let me explain this one more time. I loft the ball out over the foul line one or two boards (the eleventh or twelfth) to the left of the second arrow, all the time keeping my left foot about six boards away from the spot I'm looking at on the lane.

This system will work in some houses, but it won't in every house. That's when the men are separated from the boys—when you are forced to come up with an adjustment that will work for your specific strike shot. By way of explaining a typical adjustment, here's what I do when I find a lane on which the ball will not come in high (too heavily on the one pin or in the pocket). I'll take a few practice shots and try to hit that spot out on the lane where the ball seems to "hold back" a trifle on its way to the pocket. Then, when I'm set to release the first ball that counts, I impart a bit more lift, and when the ball hits that "hold spot" on the lane it will suddenly pick up momentum toward the pocket. Of course, there are these radical conditions, ones I hope none of you ever come up against, in which, in an effort to get away from the track—that "groove" worn in by so many thousands of games—the bowler has to belly the ball out much beyond the second arrow, sometimes even to the one and two boards. You've heard this one referred to as the "gutter shot," and there aren't very many bowlers who can play that shot consistently and score well with it.

Bowlers at the very start of their involvement in the game should be told to line their left foot up on seventeen, then toss the ball "ten to ten." That means putting the ball out over the line on the tenth board and making it cross the second arrow. Then, as their game progresses, they should start that initial two-board belly—the ball being put down on twelve, crossing ten, and then starting its arc toward the pocket.

The perfect pocket hit is when you can get the ball to drive in at about the seventeen and one-half board. This means that the arc of your ball, once it passes the ten board, will bring it back about another seven boards. Most of the great bowlers of my day and yesterday were taught the same way—that you put your ball down over ten and then make it hook seven and one-half boards into the pocket.

Suppose with that formula in mind you find that your ball is not getting up to the pocket and that it's hitting too much of the three pin. What should your adjustment be, assuming you have reached that stage of your game where you are bellying the ball two boards?

Well, it could be that the lanes are a little oily,

meaning that friction is not doing the correct job and the ball does not have enough time to make the pocket. I'd attempt to take a little speed off the shot to give it the necessary time, or I'd try to get a little more turn (lift) on the shot to make it revolve more and grab the lane. You want to take the "natural line" of each lane, because as sure as twelve strikes make a perfect game, so each lane has its own strike characteristic, a spot or area on it from which you can guide your ball into the pocket. It's our job to find that juicy spot and make it work for us, with the right amount of speed and hook. If I should slow up and still miss the head pin it means that I'm missing that sweet spot and I have to try something else, other than change of speed and more turn on release.

What I would do now is "point" the ball a bit more into that track area, which is usually between the second and third arrows (twelve to fifteen) because the ball would "bite" more in that area much earlier. Or I would move everything farther outside to get more angle on the pocket. Next time you're watching a league or professional tournament, notice how much slower than what you would call normal the bowlers are tossing the ball. Good bowlers prefer to have the oil hold the ball back somewhat so they can put more turn or rotation on the ball to help them "carry" the pins more. If I see that I've gotten nine pins and left what we call a "weak ten"—where the six went into the gutter and missed the ten—I'm usually not distressed. It tells me that I can turn the ball harder, and that even if I get a light pocket hit I'll probably knock them all down.

Before I close out this section on the strike shot, a few words of amplification on "turn" and "fingers," terms used over and over again in our sport. If you want to give your ball more time to grab the lane, to get more revolutions on the particular kind of shot you toss, you must deviate somewhat from your natural delivery. No one ever goes all out on every shot; every bowler has his own pace. But there are times when you want to be like the golfer who "lets out" with his drive, instead of just playing his normal, rhythmic shot. The bowler has to strive for a stronger effort in the wrist and fingers as he comes through the ball. It's a departure from his natural stroke, for a shot or two or twelve, if need be. If you're leaving, say, a weak ten, and you felt no adjustment was called for in your feet, you must then decide to "come through the ball" just a little harder. It'll give the ball added impetus, make it finish harder, and carry the pins better.

The ball is held at a comfortable height, equal weight on each arm as you line up with your spot. You prepare for your first step. Your shoulders and body are lined up squarely to the pins.

Into the first step—the pushaway.

Into the second step—the ball starts backward swing.

The third step—your arm is fully extended straight back in a pendulum motion.

The release and slide. Note the hand and arm have gone straight back and straight out, with the elbow in as close to the hips as possible. Notice also the slight loft of the ball.

he follow-through—your arm extends fully.

The Spare

TIME NOW TO MOVE ON to the strategies involved in spare shooting. Even though we make a resolve that nothing we throw will be anything but a strike, for sure we will be doing plenty of spare shooting. And if you never venture out of that world of the handicap league you had better make up your mind here and now that for the rest of your bowling life you'll be doing more shooting for spares than you will for strikes. Even if you get to the 190 or so stage, you can figure on making only about four or five strikes a game.

So, right now, tune in closely as I try to tell you what went wrong and what you can do right to salvage a spare from every frame you throw for the rest of your days.

When the average bowler fails to get a strike, it's almost always because he just doesn't have the savvy to do everything right. It's hard to pinpoint the trouble as being footwork or timing or accuracy. Those things come only through diligent practice over a long period of time. As I've told you, the key to high-average bowling is the ability to duplicate the right shot. If a bowler is getting one or two strikes on each of the lanes on which he's bowling and he's just a mid-average bowler, there is no concrete reason for him to change his shot. He can't be expected to make too many strikes. But if he's not getting any strikes, odds are that he's not lined up properly and he should shift.

I give myself as an example of how lining up is most important. I could come off a pair of lanes where I've just shot 250 or so and move onto another pair. Well, if my feet should go a few boards to the right and my target also move a couple of boards, I could very easily lose fifty points in that very next game. On spare shooting, however, you are almost always in a fixed position for a specific spare. All you have to do is learn certain ground rules for certain shots. The good bowler generally is in or near the pocket area, so he is shooting for the four or the ten or the four-nine split or the "bucket" (two-four-five-eight). The lower-average bowler, it seems to me, will be going mostly for spares on the right side as the result of hitting the head pin too solidly. I said spares on the right side, but I should qualify and say that those spares may very well be splits.

Let me give you something to go by when you've not gotten a strike. And again, let me caution you that these are generalizations that may or may not work. What I'm trying to instill in you is the know-how to make your own reckonings when you haven't gotten a strike and must get a spare.

Let's say you shot your ball and you failed to get it up to the head pin. Instead, you hit the three and everything went down but the one-two-four or the one-two-four-seven. Assuming you've already gotten a strike on that line, move your left foot five boards to the right and put the ball down over the target area you were playing when you got that strike. In this manner, you will bring your ball across the head pin and into the one-two pocket, the same as if you recorded a "Brooklyn" or "Jersey" strike.*

* Terms bowlers use to describe strikes recorded when the ball crosses the head pin; for example, a right-handed bowler hitting the one-two pocket or a left-handed bowler hitting the one-three pocket.

If you should leave the one-two-four-ten or the one-two-ten (washout) then you should move your feet over seven boards and still aim for the strike target. On this particular spare you are trying to hit the one pin very lightly on its left side as you face it, allowing the ball to move on into the two and four, while the one slides to the right and takes out the ten. That seven-board shift from your strike stance will get the job done, or at least get you close enough to making the spare so that you will feel that you've done a good job.

If you've left the six pin or the six-ten, then you should move over to the extreme left side of the approach and find the spot on the lane that you feel comfortable putting your ball over—by which I mean the third or fourth (center) arrow. I specify a comfortable area, because so many bowlers —and I can sympathize with them—are bugged by going over this or that marker. Find your favorite spot, then shoot accordingly. On the six-ten, many of the better bowlers will "flatten" the shot—shoot almost a straight ball at the pins to cut down the chances of chopping the six pin off the ten.

When you're shooting for single-pin spares, and most combinations, absolutely no power is required, as it is with your strike shot. You don't need a mixing ball, you don't need great revolutions on your ball. When I'm shooting for a spare, any spare, I just about "kill" my shot—I take almost everything off the ball. All you have to do to make a single-pin spare is just to tap it and it will go over. The fellow who winds up and grinds the ball and kicks high when he's shooting for spares is asking for trouble, and he's a cinch to find it when he starts missing the easy ones. Accuracy gets the spares and nothing else matters.

As a bowler progresses, he soon finds that he has a comfortable area for shooting spares, too. I've seen bowlers shooting for pins on the left side of the lane from the left side, even though most instructors advise shooting for pins on one side from the opposite side. If a bowler can get his spares while supposedly contradicting the experts, he certainly should stay with his style. As for me, I prefer to go for just about all spares by using the third arrow from the right. Maybe that's not the way other good bowlers do it, but it has worked best for me. Then, with my eyes fixed on that target area, I let my feet do the rest.

With ten pins up on the deck the spare possibilities are almost infinite. But you know as well as I do that some combinations never arise. You will always be shooting for similar combinations or one-pin spares, so you really don't have to get too involved in multiple systems for spare shooting. Obviously, if you've left only the head pin standing (a rarity), you will want to almost duplicate your strike shot, this time making sure you are more accurate. If it's the one-two or the one-two-four or the one-two-four-seven, you want the ball to go in between the one and two (we've discussed that before). If it's the one-five (the five is directly behind the one), then you also want to pretty much toss a strike ball, only you want the ball to come in a bit more solidly on the front pin so it drives right back into the five.

Naturally, if you've left pins on the right side of the lane, such as the one-three or the one-three-six, you want to toss a "strike ball," because that's the exact shot you need to fell the pins. The only difference is that there are no pins behind these to worry about. The ball will take out the one and three and the three will take out the six, which will also take out the ten, should you leave that one, too.

One of the most common spares is the two-four-five or the two-four-five-eight, commonly known as the "bucket," which occurs when you've hit too lightly on the head pin. It's a tricky one, because it requires another "pocket" hit, this time

Lining up for the 2-4-5. Move your left foot four boards to the right.

Lining up for the 1-2-4-10. Move your left foot five boards to the right.

Lining up for the 7. Move your left foot fourteen boards to the right.

Lining up for the 10. Stand on the last board with your left foot on the extreme left side of the lane.

in the pocket formed by the two and five. You
may play it the way I do, over the third arrow, but
you should shift your feet over to the right to allow for the extra distance across the lane the ball
must travel. From the center of one pin to the center of another pin there is a distance of five boards,
about five inches. But since you don't always want
your shot to hit smack in the middle of a pin,
allow for that, too. Doing what I said you should
do on the strike shot—put the ball down on a
spot about six boards from where your left foot
is placed—should give you some working formula
for spares. For those who want some basic pattern
to follow in their spare shooting I offer this one,
but you should use it only if it conforms to your
game. As I said, the way you play spares stems
from the way you shoot strikes, and no two people
really have the same equipment and game style.
At any rate, here are some guidelines for the medium-average bowler in shooting basic spares from
their normal strike zone:

> 1-2-4 or 2-4-5: Move your left foot four
> boards to the right.
>
> 1-2-4-10 or 2-4-5-8 or 8: Move your left foot
> five boards to the right.
>
> 3-6 or 3-6-10 or 3-6-9-10 or 9: Move your
> left foot five boards to the left.

3-10 or 3-9-10: Move your left foot six boards to the left.

4-9 or 4-10: Move your left foot sixteen boards to the right.

4 or 7: Move your left foot fourteen boards to the right.

6 or 10 or any split involving the 6: Stand on the last board with your left foot (extreme left side of lane) and shoot cross lane.

If you find that the formula works, stick with it. If you find that it works on too few of your spares a small adjustment will do the job, and at the same time will increase both your knowledge of the game and your enjoyment. Nothing inflates the ego of a bowler as much as making his own determinations and then finding that they really work.

You'll find that the ten-pin spare comes in for discussion more than any other one. Bowlers may tell you that this or that spare never bothers them, but don't believe a bowler when he says he doesn't fear making the ten. Even the pros come a-cropper on this one, and it makes sense that this single pin is the bane of most bowlers. To the right-hander, it means that he can make no mistake on the right, because the pin sits perched on almost the edge of the gutter. But if you follow what I say, you'll surely cut down your margin of error. Move to the far left and toss a "nothing ball." By that I mean don't try for fingers or lift. Just put the ball down over the third or fourth arrow (depending on which spot is more comfortable) and send it right into the ten. Don't try for those spine-tingling shots in which the ball scoots along the last board on the right and at the last moment comes back to hit the ten. I believe that if you can instill in yourself the thought that a drastic hook and pronounced lift aren't necessary on this shot, and if you walk straight toward your target, you will cut down on your percentage of missed spares.

I consider myself one of the best spare shooters on the tour, and I know the reason is that I don't fool around. I make shooting for spares as simple as I can, while others try to get as much stuff on their spare shots as they do on the strike ball. That's wrong, especially when you're shooting for those corner pins, such as the six or the ten or both of them. Track an imaginary line from the pin you're trying for, through the third arrow, to your eye; then, if you are square at the line and walk toward the pin or pins and toss the ball smoothly and accurately, you'll be there time after time.

To close out this segment, and to go back briefly to the strike ball, let me say this. It could be most beneficial if only you'll concentrate. Every time you go for a strike, or a spare, try to make sure that when you release the ball you are putting it down about six or seven boards away from the place you plant your left foot. You'll eliminate many of the problems that crop up if you'll follow that faithfully—sliding foot and place where ball meets lane are six to seven inches apart.

The Advanced Bowler

IF A POLL were taken among professional bowlers I suppose you'd discover that over half of them have toyed around with weight distributions in their bowling ball. Half of those who do would confess that they really didn't know why they were doing some things, and the other half would say that they're not sure that what they're doing is really helping their game. Ball weighting is rather tricky, and I do think that it's only in its infancy. If you know what you're doing and you know when to do it, varying the weights in your ball definitely will help. But I caution you—it's quite complicated.

First of all, picture imaginary lines splitting your ball from side to side and top to bottom in the area of the trademark. Those lines will separate the ball into areas of top and bottom weight, finger and thumb weight. When you want to get more weight into one of those segments you don't really add weight—you take away weight from the opposite side. As we have mentioned, the manufacturer marks on each ball he produces the spot on the weight block where dead center is located. The bowler then proceeds, by shifting the finger holes top and bottom and side to side from that dead center, to get various combinations of weight distribution. Does it sound complicated? Well, it is—terribly complicated and confusing and a risky business.

When you locate that center part of the weight block you can then proceed to implement the kind of weighting you seek. Most bowlers will endeavor to get more top weight in the ball, the idea being that top weight will delay the roll slightly by making the initial skid last longer. Favorite combinations are a quarter-ounce finger weight, a quarter-ounce side weight, and a half-ounce top weight. To show you how critical are the shifts you make as you drill into that weight block, remember at the outset that the block itself can be almost cube- or pancake-shaped. And sometimes you may not even hit the block when you drill the finger holes.

Oh, yes—the finger holes. Did someone out there ask how much weight is taken out when the holes are put in? Good question, and the answer is about two ounces, if the thumb hole was drilled to a depth of two and a half inches and the finger holes an inch shallower. Here, too, you can see the variances that will be brought into play because of finger-hole depth and width and even the initial weight of the ball.

Want to hear more? Well, the weight block doesn't always weigh the same, and in a plastic ball the block is plastic and in a rubber ball it's rubber. Sometimes, too, the density of the block is different.

→ As you get into weighting you'll learn how critical are the moves away from center and you'll be hearing things such as positive pocket weight and negative weight and other tidbits that are alternately interesting and vexing. You may even have seen some bowlers who use a ball that has a fourth hole drilled into it. There's a method to that seeming madness. One condition may call for him to take out some weight from that particular side of the ball, while another condition will cause him to plug it up. And that's what actually happens—the hole is "plugged," which means the hole is sealed off. This is done infrequently, however. Most bowlers get the job done by toting two bowling balls, differently weighted, into competition.

One last bit about the ball and the holes in them. I refer to the "pitch," the angle at which the finger holes are drilled. Some bowlers prefer that the holes go straight down, while others insist that the holes slant inward toward the center of the ball. Here, too, there are variations. Some fellows drill the finger holes on an inward angle, with the thumb outward. Others do the reverse of that. For openers, however, have the holes in your very own ball drilled straight in toward the center of the ball.

Closing out this intriguing ball-weighting subject, let me caution you that, before you mess around, know what you're doing and why you're doing it—and if you can't do it yourself, make sure that whoever is going to do it for you is eminently qualified.

And now we come to still another subject which has been the cause of much discussion and very many arguments. It's the old bit, which we touched upon earlier, about the full roller, the semiroller, or the spinner. I was taught to roll the full roller, and what it means is that the ball rolls down the lane over its widest area, with a track between the thumb and finger holes. The semiroller is a shot in which the ball travels on its merry way with the line of demarcation just below the thumb hole, and the spinner denotes that a very small surface of the ball is being used.

Many bowlers—just about all of them on the tour—have broken away from the full roller because they are now aware that the ball used in this way will not have as many revolutions as they'd like to get. Traveling over its full circumference it is only logical that the ball will have fewer turns, and that's no good. I have gotten away from the full roller, but some bowlers just cannot do it. Some fellows who can't break the habits of a lifetime can more than make up for the inability to get plenty of revolutions by becoming extremely accurate. But there is one fellow on the tour who still tries to knock down pins with that kind of shot and it no longer works for him. At one time he was almost unbeatable, but he's fallen on hard times in recent years. Part of the trouble with the full roller is the fact that much harder finishes are now used on the lanes, but that's another story, one we won't go into again.

Your thumb at nine o'clock at the point of release will produce the semi-roller.

The estimate is that over ninety percent of the nation's bowlers toss the conventional semiroller, so what's good for the masses should be good for most of us. If you operate out of that V we spoke about, and keep your thumb at about nine or ten o'clock, you will toss a semiroller. Several good bowlers have achieved good results with the spinner, but you've got to be something special to be able to rely on the shot ball after ball. It requires almost maximum turn of the wrist on release, so that the thumb, which starts out at twelve o'clock, will wind up at six o'clock on release when you give your wrist a full turn.

Many bowlers who believe they are imparting a great turn on the ball but actually aren't have lost sight of an important factor. If the thumb remains in the ball as the wrist is turned, you will get almost nothing on the shot. The hand, which started out somewhere at four o'clock, must do the turning on its own. The fellows who toss the good hook, the powerful one, are allowing the thumb to get things going, but the finished product is the result of finger action. It all happens so fast, sometimes you can't see or sense that it has happened. But it does, and only a select few bowlers will execute the job properly. For most bowlers, though, a normal wrist turn *after* the thumb vacates the ball will be more than sufficient.

A final note on this topic, a relevant one concerning "loft" and "laying it short." I'd like to get into loft, because I feel that one of the reasons I've had so much success on the tour is the fact that I've been able to get the ball out a few feet over the line with a little bounce. I have found that this allows me to get my ball into a playable track without the danger of having it go in and out if my shot starts hooking too early. Proprietors may frown on that little loft in your shot, but it really should not be that pronounced. About four or five feet out over the foul line will often keep the ball from hooking too early on lanes that are rather dry.

The corollary of the loft strategy on lanes that are slick or oily is to get the ball to start its roll almost immediately. If you were to loft the ball out too far on this kind of condition you might find that the skid and subsequent roll might deter the powerful hook you have to have. So, what you do—at least what I do—is to get the ball just a few inches out over the line, the intent being to give the ball a chance to bite into the lane while using much more of the surface. It's tricky business, but every little movement in bowling has a meaning of its own.

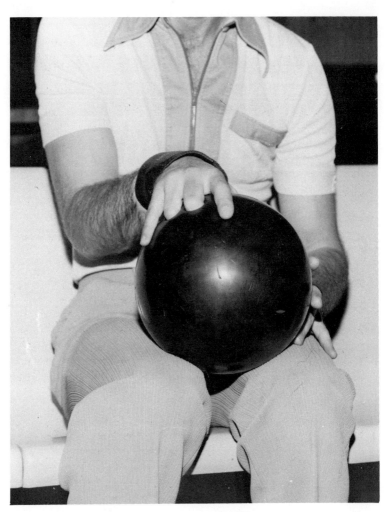

Conventional grip—finger holes drilled down approximately two and one-half inches.

Related to both ball weighting and the way you toss the ball is the way the holes are drilled in the ball. This time I don't mean weighting or width or pitch. I mean distance between the finger holes and depth of the finger holes. Naturally, when you have your first, or fifty-first, bowling ball drilled you're going to have someone who is competent at ball drilling do the job for you, unless you can do the job yourself, as so many pros do. Drilling the holes in the ball is quite a sophisticated business, and your measurements must be taken and read properly. Many a good game has been harmed by a bad job, so be careful about whom you go to.

Will you want the finger holes to go down to the conventional two and a half inches or so? Or will you want the semi-fingertip or full-fingertip grip? In the beginning, you should have deep finger holes, but later on you should use the fingertip grip. Just tell the man who does the job that you believe it's time that you moved up to the kind of ball the better bowlers use. He'll "plug" your ball, measure you once again, and then drill new holes. The charge should be a nominal one. As for the thumb hole, all bowlers try to get the thumb in as deep as they can so they can firm up their grip. Some prefer the thumb hole to be quite tight, others try for a grip that is comfortably tight.

Semi-Fingertip—finger holes drilled down about an inch and. one-half, between first finger joint and knuckle.

Comfortable sounds like a fine compromise, but many bowlers cannot get the ball to do what they want it to do unless they almost jam their thumb in.

There is a variation here, too, insofar as the fingertip grip is concerned. What some pro shops will recommend, or what some bowlers demand, is that, instead of the finger holes in a fingertip grip being drilled to an inch depth or so, the span between thumb hole and finger holes be lengthened to achieve the same thing. Elongating the distance will mean that you will be able to insert only one joint of the middle and ring fingers.

A problem that crops up with some bowlers and under some conditions is perspiring hands— and this can be a real problem. You can't get that nice feeling on your swing when you're afraid the ball may slip out of your grasp, or that you won't be able to control the shot. The thumb hole, in particular, can be a problem. To make sure that I grip the ball well each and every time, I wipe out the thumb hole before each shot. To make certain the hole is bone dry I will use a lacquer thinner or lighter fluid, both of which contain alcohol, which is a fine drying solution. As for wet hands, just about every house you bowl in is equipped with a blower built into the ball-return

Fingertip—finger holes drilled down about one inch so you will be able to insert only one joint of middle and ring fingers.

unit. You can hold your hand over the fan so that the hand will dry out, but sometimes your nerves may do you in seconds afterwards. It's a nervous condition with most, so it's a good idea to carry a towel that will absorb perspiration to the lanes with you. With some bowlers the condition is so bad that they take some kind of medication that, I guess, dries them out from within. For normal cases, though, a towel and the dryer on the ball return will be more than enough to correct the problem.

➤The same way I'd suggest that a good bowler try to use more than one bowling ball to compensate for erratic lane conditions, I'd recommend that he also have more than one pair of bowling shoes. I have three pairs, and they're constantly in use. I have one pair that has an extremely smooth sliding sole on the left foot, one that is fine for a normal approach, and another one with a rough surface. When the approaches are "unslidable" I use the first pair, and when they're too slick I'll use the last pair. There are shoes on sale that have removable Teflon-like soles, and some bowlers I know have used them. I don't use that kind and I don't intend to. Checking the soles and heels of your shoes before each shot is a surefire way of making certain they're clean. If they're not, remember that wire brush. If you suspect that the shoe on your sliding foot is too slick, you can take a little pocket knife and cut little grooves in the sole to give you a bit more traction. You'll soon discover little tricks on your own.

The temperature and the humidity in the bowling alley have a telling effect on the approaches, as well as on the lane condition we've already talked about. Be prepared for a dry, cool condition, as well as for a humid, hot one, by having more than one set of shoes with you. Do not—and I can't put too much emphasis on this—start changing your shot to a shorter or longer slide to compensate for one kind of approach as opposed to another. It'll kill your timing.

I have gone through about twenty pairs of shoes in the past five years, but I always salvage the heels from the ones I discard and use them on my next pair of new shoes after removing the new heels. I find that worn-down heels help me adjust to those tough approaches. At one time or another I have used leather soles and a leather tip on one foot, a heavier leather pad on the right sole and felt on both shoes. You'd never believe some of the combinations I have come up with just so I will not have to pull up short or go over the foul line.

Tips from the Pros

IN THESE FINAL PAGES I'd like to touch on some of the details that set the professional bowler apart from the once-in-a-while bowler and the bowler who participates in handicap leagues. Perhaps much of it will sound a bit rah-rah, but I have strong feelings about bowling and what it has done for me and what it can do for you and everyone else if you give it a fair chance.

I like to fancy myself as a cool customer at all times, and I suppose lots of people consider me to be just that. I work at that image all the time because I feel strongly that you can only be what you want to be. Maybe I have felt a tremor of excitement in some pressure situations, but I believe that desire can neutralize the emotions that could upset your game. When I won the Miller Open title in Milwaukee my father was in the audience and I could sense how tense he was. It made me feel a little up tight, too, but I counterbalanced that by just resolving to play my shot, play my game. It worked, all right, but I'd put that little episode at the top of my list if I had to name my most emotional experience on the lanes. It was the first time he'd been at a tournament, and I feel proud that I rolled a 300 game with him looking on, with that heart machine strapped to me, and that I went on to take the championship. Second place might have been okay for some people, but I knew that victory was all that mattered, at least on that day. I came down to the final two frames needing strikes to win—and I got them.

If I had to name the most vital aspect of the game for the pro bowler, it's the ability to find the track on each lane. It's quite a science, knowing where the track is and then knowing if it's a playable one. Bowlers have spent years and tears attempting to be able to read lanes. Even when they think they finally have gotten a book on a lane, they might be distressed to learn that someone else saw that particular lane entirely differently. But to be a good bowler, you must be able to learn to read the lanes.

Initially, we like to know where the oil has been put down. Many houses will oil gutter to gutter, right across the lane, while others will dress the lanes from "five to five," which means that the outside five boards on each side are dry compared to the inside boards. In the latter case it's easy for the pro to find his way to the pocket. He just gets his shot in the dry area and the ball will miss the track, which is in the neighborhood of ten to fifteen, and take a true course to the one-three. If the track is within the "legal" area—if it's not so deep as to radically affect the ball—by all means try to get your ball to go into the track. If it's a deep track, then the path of the ball will not be a true one and you'll struggle. Most of the pros will come into a house—and don't forget that we bowl in a different center each week—and immediately start playing between the second and third arrow. We know that's where the track is, and that all that remains is to determine if it's a playable one.

If you've watched us bowl in some houses where the track was so rutted and grooved as to make a good shot impossible, you've no doubt seen us playing "inside." That means we are putting the ball over the third and fourth (center) arrows in an effort to circumvent the track.

The kind of track we like is the normal one, where the ball will grab a bit and allow you to make your best shot. That's the time you see scoring swing to the high side out on the tour, because most of the pros have all the other facets of the game down pat and all they want is the ball to get a fair chance at taking the route to the pins that they planned for it.

I went, in a superficial way, into the problem of sore fingers earlier. The very fact that there are so many preparations and gloves and remedies on the market for sore fingers ought to indicate that there probably is no way to eliminate the trouble. With the thumb working all alone on its side of the ball, it figures that it will bear the brunt of the pressure. Look at the bowling hand of anyone who bowls as many games as I do, and has been for some years, and it's a certainty that the bowling thumb will be much larger than the other one— and that it will be very much callused from all the abuse it takes. My guess is that about one-fifth of the field in any given PBA event suffers from some kind of thumb or finger woe during or after the tournament. All right, you ask, what can one do to keep those bowling balls flying and not allow finger problems to hurt your game?

The callus I have on my thumb is there by design—by which I mean that it happens to almost all of us and it helps ward off cuts and bruises. But I also keep a callus file in my equipment bag and I "manicure" the callus regularly to make sure it doesn't get too big. The callus should keep you from cutting the thumb, but some bowlers always experience some difficulty and take measures before taking to the lanes. A fellow like Barry Asher always "dresses" his thumb with court plaster or some other kind of cut inhibitor before shooting a block of games. Don't forget that we are professionals and for many of us it's our only livelihood. A severely bruised or bleeding finger or thumb may force you to withdraw from a big-money event. You could go on, I guess, with a bad thumb or whatnot, but then you're like a prize fighter trying to win a bout when he's hurt one or both of his hands. There's no way.

Bowlers who are prone to hand injury, or those who have cut open their thumb, or finger, can bathe the digit in a solution that will encourage healing, but there's no guarantee that it will work. I have tried it, and have heard that others have also used a zinc oxide preparation the night before a block of games to close up a gaping wound. It works, but there's no telling for how long.

Early in 1971, when I was experiencing some trouble after having been named Bowler of the Year in 1970, I was trying all sorts of different releases and balls in an attempt to get my game back on the beam. In the two days prior to the start of a tournament in Waukegan I rolled nearly one hundred games. Well, I did away with some of the problems in my game, but I developed a new one. The combination of releases and different grips did one heckuva job on my fingers. I was hurting, but bowling well, as the event unfolded, but after a couple blocks the pain in my swollen thumb got so bad I had to withdraw. What made it so tough to swallow was the fact that I was in third place at the time. It may have cost me a few thousand dollars, but I was beginning to lose feeling in the thumb and I didn't want to hurt myself so badly that it could have put my bowling career in jeopardy.

Bowlers who have experienced or are fearful of injuries have their own remedies. One bowler, Jack Biondolillo, used to soak his whole hand in ice water, thinking that he would freeze away the pain. Don Johnson has been known to insert an occasional sore thumb into a raw potato. In fact, when Don won the U.S. Open early in 1972 he went through about five grooved potatoes during the last two days of the competition. He claimed that the starch drew out the pain. Zinc oxide, however, which is the base ingredient, I am told, in those baby ointments, seems to do the best job in closing gaping wounds or healing cuts.

When should I purchase a new ball? This is a question put to me quite often by bowlers who seem to feel that because they see a "track" on the ball's surface after rolling down the lane so many times, the ball has lost its value. Scratch marks will appear on the ball after a while and they'll show up much sooner on an amateur's bowling ball than a pro's. The reason is simple. Most bowling centers condition their lanes to accommodate league bowlers or those who are just out for a day's fun. Too much oil on the lanes is the bane of the low- or medium-average bowler because he can't get his ball to hook. Less oil, more scratch marks—very simple.

Once you get to the high-average leagues, or into the professional ranks, you will find a need for each kind of ball. One on which there are scratch marks, or a definite track, will be fine for slick lanes. On dry lanes a ball with a smooth surface might be called for. Then, too, there are different kinds of ball surfaces to begin with. You can roll a couple dozen games with one of the plastic balls before you even see the beginnings of a track, while on softer rubber models the track may show up after as little as one game.

Just remember that a new ball will usually slide much more than one that has been in use, and that unless you take your game to the upper echelons it won't matter very much what kind you use. Of course, if the track gets so noticeable that you can't get most of it out in the ball-polishing machine in most centers, it may be time for you to think about a new ball. You wouldn't want to finally get your game down really pat and then find that the ball you've been using is hurting your "carry" at the other end.

Professionals always try to strike a happy medium with the ball. They want one that won't grab too much, and yet will roll and then carry well. In my big year of 1971, when I won four championships, I used just one bowling ball all year. If you look in the record book you'll see that I shot about one thousand competitive games in the PBA alone. Rather than change my ball to fit into a situation, I just changed my shot instead. I have the ability to change my shot quite a bit, and there are only a few others who seem to be able to do so. A pro like Dave Soutar can make drastic alterations in his game, but another one, like Don Johnson, one of the best, cannot seem to toss the ball hard as some of us do. So my assumption is that Don changes balls quite a bit; I don't have to.

With the lane finishes being what they are today, I now carry two bowling balls, one rubber and the other plastic. The reasons I do so I explained a while ago. Plastic will make the ball slide more before going into its roll, while the rubber ball will grip sooner. That's about the only concession I'll make. I like to think that I can beat any other problem with the correct speed and accuracy.

Staying on the new versus old ball theme, I'd like to point out that many a bowler has bought a new one or plugged up an old one in the belief that his fingers or his grip have changed. It may be that a bowler who weighed 250 who went on a diet and lost 75 pounds may have lost some "finger weight," but why go to the expense and bother of a plug job? Often a strip of tape or a piece of cork in the thumb hole or finger hole will offset the problem. There are many items on the market to give you a better grip on the ball, and you should try one or a combination of them.

Many of the pros insert strips of tape or cork in the ball's holes at the start of the day, and as the day wears on, or as humidity increases and the thumb also increases, they will remove the strips to keep the grip comfortable. Try this method before you run out and spend those hard-earned dollars for a new ball or a plugging. If we, the pros, employ this trick, surely it will work for you.

It might be oversimplification to close out an instructional book with advice on practice, but the "practice makes perfect" credo has been the one I have followed and believe in. This is an age of specialization in the world of athletics as well as in the business world. If you work at a job thirty or forty hours a week—whether it's bowling or business—you just can't cut corners when "business hours" are over. My every waking moment is spent in thoughts of bowling, and while no one ever reaches the pinnacle of perfection, I never ever let up in trying to get there.

I have heard bowlers state that there is no reason to practice when they're doing well. That's backward thinking. When I'm bowling well I practice all the more, because I believe that's the time to embed good habits in my mind. Bowling is a grind-out, and you should grind all the good things into your memory. Study the words I've set down, then go out there and practice . . . practice . . . practice.

NELSON BURTON JR.

Nelson Burton Jr. was born into a bowling family. His father, Nelson Burton Sr., is in the Bowling Hall of Fame. The author, at the age of sixteen, bowled his first of many perfect games. Now at the age of thirty, he has won the ABC singles, doubles, and team events. He has also won ten PBA tournaments and in 1970 was voted Bowler of the Year. He has been an All-American six times and holds the record for the highest three-game score in tournament competition: 869, on games of 279—300—290.

The author is also a bowling proprietor in St. Louis, where he lives with his wife, Sissy, and young daughter, Trina. He owns and pilots his own plane.

JERRY LEVINE

Jerry Levine, a former reporter, is the publicity coordinator for the Professional Bowlers Association.